Ancient Truths

© Brian Mgabazi

BRIAN MGABAZI

Ancient Truths

Copyright © 2020 Brian Mgabazi

Published by Brian Mgabazi Ministries

ISBN: 978-1-77925-295-1

Dedication

Dedicated to the Holy Spirit and to my Wife Blessing and Our children for whom I love with my life. Girls you are my world, you my love and you, my life. May the Good Lord continue to guide you and that you may walk in greatness, in power and in love.

CONTENTS

Acknowledgments   i

Introduction...   Page 6

Chapter 1   Ancient Ways...   Page 9

Chapter 2   Ancient Ways;
               Principle of Money...   Page 28

Chapter 3   Ancient Ways:
               Seeds Principle...   Page 37

Chapter 4   Ancient Ways: Power of Pain...   Page 49

Chapter 5   Ancient Ways: Wisdom...   Page 56

Chapter 6   Ancient Mountains...   Page 68

Chapter 7   Ancient Ways: Altars...   Page 80

Chapter 8   Ancient Landmarks...   Page 105

Chapter 9   Ancient Truth...   Page 115

Chapter 10   Ancient Truth: The Kingdom
               The Power and The Glory...   Page 121

Acknowledgments

Many people have been so supportive and have stood with me as I wrote this book. Some have helped in editing it and getting this book where it is right now. I would like to thank my dearest wife Blessing for standing with me, all my friends for the unwavering prayer support.

Introduction

As the young preacher stood up and there was a sense of euphoria and expectancy in the crowd, it was as if you could physically grab it, as this young but eloquent and charismatic young man was considered arguably one of the best preachers, we had in our denomination then. With excitement and exuberance, he opened his mouth, the first statement that came out of his mouth instantaneously clouded the atmosphere, and it became serene, tense and dampened by just that one statement. He had just said "I believe God did not create man but man created God", and well he did then spend the next thirty minutes trying to defend his theological view point. To say the least that day sealed the coffin over his public ministry in our church.

They are established doctrinal views that won't change no matter what, they are what they are and should not and cannot be changed. No matter how so much the young man tried to defend his view the elated preaching ended up a dumb squid because the young man didn't stick to established doctrinal line, he deviated from ancient truth.

There are certain things that change all the time as life is versatile and dynamic. All the same there are things that do not at all change and will never change no matter what. There were like that generations ago and will always be the same till time immemorial. The Gospel seems to be shifting over the years but all the same there are certain fundamentals that remain constant. There are beliefs and revelatory thoughts and statements that will come over time but the fact that will stand forever.

This book takes a look at some of these ancient truths that have sustained life, people, families, ministries, marriages and the universe. We delve into universal kingdom laws, kingdom principles and teachings that are meant to help us and build us.

To dig deeper into these ancient truths, we went into the law of first mention and we delved deeper into the word of God and searched for scriptures that have verses that has the word ancient mentioned. The bible has a number of things that it mentions as being ancient. We will dig into some of these so we can then establish the ancient Truths that build us.

Here is a list of some of the things mentioned in the bible as ancient. The word ancient is mentioned many times in the word of God and as such has become the basis of our research and teaching. The word ancient is then associated with these number of verses in the scriptures.

1.   Ancient ways/Paths

2.   Ancient mountains

3.   Ancient men Ezekiel 9:6

4.   Ancient prophets

5.   Ancient rivers

6.	Ancient Times

7.	Ancient Things

8.	Ancient Wisdom

9.	Ancient Landmarks

10.	Ancient Kings

11.	Ancient of Days Daniel 7: 9,13,22

12.	Ancient People

13.	Ancient Priests Jeremiah 19:1

14.	Ancients of Gebal & wise men Ezekiel 27:9

15.	Ancient High Places Ezekiel 36 vs. 2

We will from this list establish certain truths that will help us develop wisdom so we can go to the next level. The Word ancient by itself establishes a truth to be antique, to be established right from the beginning.

Key thing about antiques is that they are expensive, they are priceless in most cases and they are there for time immemorial. We look into these matters.

God bless as you read this book.

CHAPTER ONE

ANCIENT TRUTH: ANCIENT PATHS

My first Sunday main service preaching engagement was in the year 1989 I was still a small boy living in the farming town of Mvurwi in Zimbabwe. My late father was a banker and my mum ran a flea market stall. We were from an average family that had a good standing in the community. My mum had given her life to the Lord in 1976 coincidentally being the same year I was born. My father though a believer never went to church, but daily he commanded us with military precision to go to church, my mum was an astute believer who without fail attended church religiously. She taught us to live in the word of God and at all cost made sure we were brought up in the ways of the LORD.

My maternal grandmother Evelyn Mutasa whom I loved dearly with all my heart and has since gone to be with the Lord grew up teaching me nothing else but the word. The book of Ezekiel being her favorite, I remember the first scripture that she made to memorize:

"Son of Man prophesy unto these mountains of Israel, and say your mountains of Israel, hear the word of the Lord". Ezekiel 36 vs. 1

In a way I believe as I recited this scripture this marked the beginning of my journey into ministry. Growing up I was surrounded by nothing except the word of God, and I had my first encounter with the Lord Jesus Christ on an ordinary day. I do recall I was playing and pretending that I was preaching, I was doing what I had seen a famous evangelist in those days, who later founded, Ambassador for Christ Church. He would jump from the podium and shout Zimbabwe is my pulpit. I had taken my mum's big laundry dish and turn it upside down and was using it as my makeshift pulpit and was jumping from there and I was shouting Zimbabwe is my pulpit imitating Evangelist Abel Sande.

In an open vision that afternoon I looked and I saw The Lord Jesus Christ come down and he started to speak to me. My Aunt who was present saw all this and was astounded at what was happening. That became the day of my separation as God called me into ministry. Growing up as a family we were members of ZAOGA FIF, though at some point we left ZAOGA and became members of Apostolic Faith Mission in Zimbabwe which is where I got baptized. ZAOGA FIF was an amazing church where we had such a fascinating time, key being that as youth we were given opportunity to exercise our gifts and also had a chance to preach. As a boy of fourteen (14), I had my first chance to preach on Sunday in the main service. I remember a friend and mentor now District pastor in ZAOGA FIF Pastor Gerald Veva had given me a cassette of a preaching by the now late Evangelist R.W Shambach and I had listened to this message over a hundred times on my walk man cassette player. I stood up one Sunday after being given an opportunity to preach and I remember preaching that message by Brother R.W Shambach which I now knew verbatim. The message was on the Hebrew boys Shadrack, Meshack and Abednego.

When I did the altar call, I had several people that came for prayer. The first lady that spoke to me said she had an operation that was scheduled for the next for appendicitis. I prayed for the Lady and the next day the doctors could not do the operation the appendix had healed all the pain was gone. I prayed for the next lady who had been given six months to live because she had developed cancer, God healed her instantly. This was the year 1989 and as I write this book it's the year of our Lord 2020, both ladies are alive and totally healed.

There was a move of God in that service that brought healing. God didn't look at the age of the preacher he just honored his word, because he only watches over his word and he performs his word. There are established facts of how God moves and what he does and how he does things that cannot and will not change no matter what. It's believed that time will change and transform some things, but the fact is that certain things will never change no matter what. There are things that will never change no matter what because God meant them to be that way and they remain what they are. There are many things that the scriptures have established and they will remain that way forever and ever.

I have been to different churches and countries that do have different ways in which they do things but all the same there are certain biblical truths that are well established that will not change in spite of disputes in interpretation and views on the subject. We will look at several of these subjects, it's some but not all as they are too long on the list. There are ways that are ancient that God has honored, respected and has always fulfilled.

These ways have never changed and will never change no matter what. I will look at some of these ways and will try to establish the ancient ways of God. Just as God honored the preaching of a small fourteen-year-old boy and healed people, he still will honor his word. God is watching over his word and he will perform it.

Tithe and Offering

The debate on the issue of tithe and offerings has from time immemorial been there. The fact still remains that God is a God who works on principles of giving and receiving. Right from the Old Covenant to the New

Covenant God has always been a giver and as he is so are we. We will explore two words that are tithe and offering. The first mention of the word tithe is in the book of Genesis,

"And blessed be the highest God, which has delivered your enemies into thy hand and he gave him tithes of all". *Genesis 14 vs. 20*

Abraham who is our father in faith became the first man to give a tithe of all. He gave his tithe to Melchizedek who was a priest and a King. This established the precedent of the tithe principle. The fact that Abraham gave a tithe out of faith establishes that tithe isn't a law but it is of faith.

Second mention of the word tithe is

"And all tithe of the land, whether of the seed of the land, or of the fruit of the tree, is the Lords; it's holy unto the LORD". Leviticus 27 vs. 30

Tithe is then established that it belongs to the LORD. The fact that God establishes this word that tithe is his means he wants us to pay our tithe as a matter of principle. All tithe weather of seed or of fruit belongs to the Lord. Then it is established that it is holy. If its holy any man that then does not honor the Holy things of God has issues

The last scripture to talk of tithes in the bible is in Hebrews,

"And as I may so say, Levi also paid tithes in Abraham"
Hebrews 7 vs. 9

For a doctrine to be established there is need to have three or more scriptures that support it as scripture interprets scripture. Tithe is then even established as a principle that is mentioned in the New Testament teachings especially in the book of Hebrews which is the book of faith.

The first mention of the word OFFERING is

"And in the process of time it came to pass, that Cain brought of the fruit of the ground an offering unto the Lord and Abel, he also brought of the firstlings of his flock and of the fat thereof. And the LORD had respect unto Abel and his offering". Genesis 4:3 – 4

The fact that is established is that God had respect for the offering of Abel because it was the first fruit. It wasn't just an offering but it was the principle of the first. God will respect a person's offering based on whether it was given as the first and with a whole heart. The two brothers both gave an offering, but the offering of Cain wasn't accepted but that of Abel was acceptable to the Lord. The reason being Abel gave the first. Most people give the last or the middle to God they never give the first. The fact that the church has received the offering doesn't mean that God has received it. It's imperative that we give the first to God.

It is interesting that even non-Christians have been able to live by these principles, a man like Bill Gates the founder of Microsoft gives away nothing less than five (5) billion United States dollars yearly. They call it philanthropy as they give to the poor and to worthy causes. Lately most companies have adopted this ancient truth and they call it Corporate Social Responsibility. It has become such a big thing that even the government is giving tax rebates for such giving. It started with God who gave his only begotten son and it's an established truth, Giving to God can never be substituted for anything. We must give to the Lord as he gives us, we give back to him.

Prayer and Fasting

The third principle that we will look at is fasting and prayer,

"Howbeit this kind goes not out but by prayer and fasting'. Mathew 17 vs. 21

Prayer and fasting are principles that are so established in scripture right from genesis to revelation. You cannot replace this one with anything. Prayer is a principle that works. Jesus prayed, Abraham the father of faith prayed there are just things that will not change.

"Abraham prayed unto God: and God healed Abimelech, and his wife and his maid servants; and they bear children". Genesis 20 vs. 17

The healing of Abimelech was premised on the prayers of Abraham. The manifestation or lack of manifestation there of is usually because of a lack of prayer or prayerfulness thereof.

The first principle that we learn about Abraham is that he was a man of prayer. His life I established by prayer and in prayer. Prayer is the very answer to challenges of life. Abraham's prayer brought two things to Abimelech, one that is healing and two it brought fruitfulness, the realm of prayer has the capacity to bring healing to any sick person and the realm of prayer will bring manifestation of fruitfulness. Prayer is irreplaceable no matter what. We have a generation that looks for shot cuts to victory and ministry, this generation is then in a place where they are struggling because they are not staying in prayer. Prayerless Christians are powerless Christians. Whenever you have a Christian who doesn't spend time with God you already know that the Christian isn't going anywhere. Hannah is the most talked about woman when it comes to prayer. Hannah pushed in prayer till the heavens opened up. She prays a prayer that's coming from deep inside those forces the heavens to react.

"And she was in bitterness of soul, and prayed unto the Lord, and wept sore" 1 Samuel 1 vs. 10

Hannah prayed and her prayers. Prayer is a way to get answered. Though she prayed and it seems God wasn't hearing her, she kept on pushing and praying until God manifested the answers to her prayers. So many people take prayer as a religious thing, they don't push in prayer till results manifest. There is a proclivity to take prayer as one of the important things but we must know prayer is the important thing.

"And the lord turned the captivity of Job, when he prayed for his friends: the LORD gave Job twice as much as he had before". Job 42 vs. 10

This is the power of prayer, it can bring restoration, revival, recovery and restitution. To note is that Job wasn't praying for himself, he was interceding for his friends the very friends who were telling him to curse God and die. Prayer is a spiritual exercise. There is an ability to bring manifestation, bringing the heavens on the earth by reason of prayer. Jesus being God still prayed unto his father. He understood that his relationship with his father was based on his prayer life.

"And in the morning, rising up a great while before day, he went out and departed into a solitary place and there prayed". Mark 1 vs. 35

"And he withdrew himself into the wilderness and prayed" Luke 5 vs. 16

Jesus in the beginning was with God, he was God but all the same he prayed and God heard his prayers. The fact that he was equal to God didn't stop him from praying to God, He understood that all things need prayer and all things move only by prayer. Jesus then did spend time in the place of prayer. Jesus was always withdrawing himself from public ministry so that he may refill himself.

"Peter therefore was kept in prison: but prayer was made without ceasing of the church unto God for him". Acts 12 vs. 5

Peter has been arrested and imprisoned, the church calls for prayer. They without ceasing prayed. God causes an Angel to come and open the prison doors and peter walked out of that place and was drawn to the house where they were praying.

Someone once said to me one hour of public ministry requires that you withdraw yourself into prayer for eight hours. Don't be a person that is always pouring our but you don't have God pouring into you. The amount of ministry that you are pouring out must be anchored in prayer otherwise you will have fatigue and you will have demonic attacks that you are not able to handle. The years 1993 to 1995 I was doing my Advanced Level Certificate. These years became the formative stage of my ministry as I began to spend so much time in prayer and fasting. I had connected to Pastor Gerald Veva who began to mentor me in the area of prayer. We would fast Monday to Friday and then pray from 12 mid-day to 1600 hours then from 21:00 hours to 02:00 hours in the morning.

Spending so much time in the presence of God can transform any man from being an ordinary man to being the supernatural man. I began to hear God on a level I had only read about in books, I began to see the power of God on such a level as I had only desired but never thought possible. In the season of prayer my eyes were opened to the realms of the supernatural so much that I knew things before they happened. I could be on the way to church and I would have an open vision of what would happen in church. I got to an extent of being home and I get a word and though there was a preplanned program I knew when I get to church it would be changed so that I can preach.

Prayer is the undisputable power that can change and transform anything. If there is a man to pray there is a God to answer. In the year 2008 I was based in the Eastern Highlands of Zimbabwe and there I was part and parcel of New Life Ministries. The Now Late Bishop Bismark Senior father to the honorable Bishop Tudor Bismark came and released me to start a ministry. I went into a prayer season, and as I prayed, I would spend three days and nights in the mountains. After a season of nearly six months of these nonstop prayers, God spoke to me to start our Church, Covenant Life Ministries International.

We started in our first service with six people then moved to 14 by the third service, then 21 people then 35 people. It's amazing that the church kept growing in leaps and bounds. We never held a crusade; we never advertised but the church grew. I knew the growth was supported by prayer. Its prayer that has the ability to pull people and establish a church.

The reason why most pastors end up going to witch doctors for power or people is because they are simply lazy to pray. You can never replace prayer with anything else. There is a price of prayer to be paid for the manifestation of power to happen.

Honor and Respect

The forth Principle that we want to establish of ancient ways is the principle of Honor and respect. It's amazing how the world has so much moved and people have lost respect of things they must honor.

"As snow in summer, and rain in harvest, so honor is not seemly for a fool". Proverbs 26 vs. 1

The statement that you cannot receive from what you don't honor is very true. What you honor will bring a harvest for you. Its only fools that don't understand that the greatest seed any man can pay is a seed of honor.

"He that receives a prophet in the name of a prophet shall receive a prophet's reward; and he that receives a righteous man in the name of a righteous man shall receive a righteous man reward". Mathew 10 vs. 41

Honor is a seed that must be given; honor must be given to whom honor is due. Lack of honor will shorten your life. There is a reward to honor, when it's not given then honor will not produce a reward,

Honor must be given to a number of people and things

a) Your Mother and father must receive honor,

"Because God said, you are to honor your father and your mother, and whosoever curses father or mother must certainly be put to death". Mathew 15 vs. 4

We have a generation that things because they are more learned than their parents therefore, they must not honor them. Your parent is your life source and as such what they say carry weight and God will honor. If they curse you that curse will stand the reason, being they are the source of your life. Most struggles people have been because they lack a parental blessing. The reason of the fight between Esau and Jacob is not the wealth of their father but the blessing of their father. The words that the father is speaking is what is more important than the wealth that the father has. It's imperative that children should honor their parents, part of that honor is taking care of their parents and listening to their words.

b) Honor Jesus Christ

"So that everyone may honor the son as they honor the father. Whoever does not honor the son does not honor the father who sent him". John 5 vs. 23

c) You honor your body by living right and not engaging in sexual immorality. Sexual immorality includes sexual orgies, adultery, fornication, incest, bestiality, pornography and homosexuality.

"For this reason, God delivered them to sexual impurity as they followed the lusts of their hearts and dishonored their bodies with one another". Romans 1 vs. 24

Most people do not honor their bodies that's why they eat anything and live anyhow. The greatest challenge mist people have is that they do not look over their own bodies. The only thing that's carrying your spirit, your vision, your dreams and all your ministry is the body. The body has so much that it has that we take it for granted. The only reason God is still answering your prayers is because you still in the body. The moment your spirit leaves your body then even God can't hear your prayers. The body is so powerful that if its dies then all things will die with it.

d) Honorable people must get honor.

"Pay everyone whatever you owe them- taxes to whom taxes are due, tolls to whom tolls are due, fear to whom fear is due, and honor to whom honor is due." Romans 13 vs. 7

By reason of wealth or position and title they are honorable. The members of parliament are called by a title Honorable by reason of their positions. There are people that must be honored by reason that they have attained certain places or positions in life. It's important to honor and respect people by reason of what they become in life as other people have failed to attain that in life.

e) Honor Widows who have nobody to look after them. 1 Titus 5 vs. 3 "Honor widows who have no other family members to care for them". Honor them because God is the husband of the widows. By failure to honor them you fail to honor God.

f) Marriage must be honored.

"Let marriage be kept honorable in every way and the marriage bed undefiled. For God will judge those that commit sexual sins, especially those who commit adultery." Hebrews 13 vs. 4

This is definitely one area that this generation does not want to hear. They will do everything to avoid this subject but the bible is straight forward. Marriage must be honored at all cost. Sexual relationships outside the marriage will bring God's judgment. Marriage is an example of the relationship between Christ and the church, it therefore must be honored at all costs. A lot of people have no honor for the institution of marriage that's why they will go and try to get into relationships with married man or women. It's important to honor what God honors.

g) Pastors, Elders, Overseers and Bishops who lead in the Church must be given not just honor but double honor.

"Let the elders that rule well be counted worthy of double honor, especially those who labor in the word and in teaching". 1 Titus 5 vs. 17

Double honor is interesting, because it talks about making sure what you do to those outside you do double for those in the house of the LORD. Honor them with giving them a good position to sit and give them a food wage.

h) You must honor all that are older to you in age, position.

Honor is usually lost because people fail to recognize the gift and fail to see that what's before them is from God. Viewing people should be from the eyes of God. See people as God see them. View people from the lenses of God.

"And Jesus said unto them, A prophet is not without honor, save in his own country, and among his own kin, and in his own house". Mark 6 vs. 4

People easily become familiar with people in their circles and people around them. People become familiar with people because they spend too much time with them. It's easy to lose respect and honor for someone because you are just looking at them from the surface. Honor is shown by a number of things;

• The seat you allocate a person shows your honor for them.

• Quality or quantity of your gift or service shows your honor, you can never give to a president a usd2.00 gift because quality and quantity is important.

• Honor is revealed by doing the very thing that is asked of you and your reaction and action to those things. Delayed obedience is disobedience, do what is asked of you when it's asked of you otherwise you are showing disobedience.

• Listening and walking according to the words of God.

• Honorarium is money that is given as a gift to a preacher; it is given to honor the gift and the anointing on the Men. The amount shows honor, as men give according to how much they honor the man never according to what they have. If an Arch Bishop or a prophet comes into a place, people will go all way out to give a gift to him. The amount or the quality shows how much people respect the man.

One Man and One woman is the sixth ancient truth that we will explore. God's original intent with marriage was one man one woman. It's a fact that was established right from the beginning God created Adam and Eve and these two became the first man and wife. There wasn't one man and two women but one man and one woman.

"Let the deacons be the husbands of one wife" 1 Titus 3 vs. 12

It is therefore a fact that nobody in leadership should ever be in a polygamous marriage. If any man chooses that path, they should leave leadership. Man over time perverted the plans and purposes of God. Men have been so much into his own ways that he has lost the plan that God had. The intention of God has always been one man should have one wife Adam and Eve.

The last one we will deal with is holiness.

"What shall we say then? Shall we continue in sin, that grace may abound" Romans 6 vs.1

As much as we preach grace, we must also preach holiness.

It's important for us to live a holy life as the word says be holy as I am holy. Righteousness is given to us by the very fact that we have received Jesus Christ as our lord and savior. Holiness is something we work towards to attain. We are living in a grace generation that believes we still can sin and be in the Church. I have met preachers that will be coming from committing fornication and come and preach. The demons will come out the people will be healed. But the fact remains at the end-of-life judgment will begin in the house of the Lord. We cannot continue to sin for grace to abound. Holiness cannot be replaced or substituted by anything.

CHAPTER TWO

ANCIENT TRUTH: MONEY PRINCIPLE

The young man was on top of the world, he had suddenly come into a windfall of over three hundred thousand dollars (300 000. 00) USD. The first thing he did was buy designer clothes, he went into designer furniture and top of the range car. Within a week the money had dwindled to one hundred thousand dollars (150 000) USD. His lifestyle changed and as I spoke to him to invest in property, he didn't get me as he felt he was now very rich.

Three years down the line, the young man was back where he had started, the cars were gone, and the moveable property gone. He is living from hand to mouth. The main reason being when money came, he didn't have a plan. There was no set strategy on how to save, invest and spend. Most people are like this young man. They have not mastered the art of money. They have not taken time to learn the principles of money.

Most people blame demons for their failure in life whilst it's just simply a lack of strategic thinking that brought them to where they are. Someone said to me long back "Money loves the comfort of a structure". If you don't put a structure money will fail to come or if it does flow your way it will eventually just disappear. Most people do not build their capacity to handle money. They remain in the 100-dollar zone. That's why when money comes, they will squander it all, when they are left with a few hundred they suddenly are looking for ways to multiply the hundred, when they were in thousands, they never thought of that. The issue is capacity. They remain a seven-ton bridge whilst the road is now a 30-ton road and eventually they will collapse under the weight of what they are trying to carry. Money is a good tool but a bad master. If you can use money, you can be great but if it uses you then you will suffer.

"A feast is made for laughter, wine makes merry: but money answers all things". Ecclesiastes 10 vs. 19

Money is a necessity for all things to happen, but money has its own principles that will make it come and that make it stay, no matter what these principles will not change. The Jewish people have several beliefs on the issue of wealth and money, these are some but not all. We will look at some of the Jewish beliefs about wealth and money.

Poverty is a result of poor choices not bad luck. Poverty is seen by many as a lack of money, but poverty in reality is simply a lack of strategic thinking. Poverty is a result of poor choices in life, poor choices in investments, poor choices in spending. If anyone is to make money the key is in changing the choices that they make. People think that bad luck is the reason they are poor. Most people make a series of bad money decisions that will result in them being in poverty. Majority of people never get schooled in the art of making money, the science of keeping money and the mindset of how to spend it.

Money must only be saved, given away and invested and must never be squandered. In life I have seen that anyone who has ever won the lotto or had a sudden windfall have all ended up poor and without anything. The main reason is they have never learned the principle of saving and investment. The best way to raise money to invest is by saving. Squandering money is one thing that is so visible in communities of poor people. The poor buy branded clothes, shoes, trainers and all sorts of things. Poor people spend lots of money on useless things, they squander money but rich people invest money before they spend it.

The best investment that any man can do is investment in land and property; it's the best investment that the rich people do. Arrogance is Knowledge minus wisdom. The reason people lose money or never make money is a result of arrogance. The fact that you have knowledge isn't enough, you must be able to apply that knowledge. Wisdom is the right application of knowledge. The world is full of sports coaches, marriage coaches but doesn't have enough financial coaches People need to be coached on how to make money, how to save money and how to invest money. Every kingdom is only as powerful as the resources it can gather. This is true of politics, true of churches, true of businesses and all facets of life and ministry.

What's important is what you spend not what you earn. As much as you can earn a million dollars but if you spend two million you will always be in a hole. What you earn doesn't matter, because you can earn 100dollars and begin to save 20 dollars and within five years be an owner of a big business. It's building on the principle that works.

Money is a need and we cannot do without it. Money is currency; the word currency ultimately means flow. Which means money flows and as it flows it has its own principles that make it flow in a certain direction.

How to pull Money;

- Learn all that you can about money

• What you desire and respect will come to you, same principle applies to money. There are people who have so little regard for money and money does escape them.

• Have an eye that can see opportunities and money will flow to you.

• Tithe and God will open the windows of heaven and pour you out a blessing with no room to contain it.

"Bring ye all the tithes into the storehouse that there may be meat in mine house, and prove me now says the LORD of HOSTS, and see if I will not open the windows of heaven, and pour you out a blessing, that there shall not be room enough to receive it". Malachi 3 vs. 10

• Be a giver as the word is straight forward.

"Give and it shall be given unto you good measure, pressed down, shaken together and running over, shall men give into your bosom. For with the same measure that you use so shall it be measured unto you" Luke 6 vs. 38

Why you need Money

"Money is a defense", Ecclesiastes 7 vs. 12, 10 vs.19.

Most people are in a precarious situation because they have no money. Money can buy you all the freedom you want. Most people in prison lacked just money to pay their way out of the crimes they committed. The biggest criminals are out and enjoying the world simply because they do have the resources to get the best lawyers in the world. Poverty makes you vulnerable, you drive what you don't love, you eat what you don't enjoy, and you sleep in places that are not secure and conducive simply because you don't have the resources.

"Money answers all things" Ecclesiastes 10:19.

Money has all the answers to life. Money will give you all you need. It has the ability to buy you the future. There are things that will never be answered by prayer, they are answered by money. If there is no money, they will eventually be a shut down. No matter how much anointed a person is if there is no money their ministry will amount to nothing. Money will make the gospel move.

Money builds a memorial and can change the mind of God.

'And when he looked on him, he was afraid and said, what is it LORD, and he said unto him, your prayers and your alms have come up as a memorial before God" Acts 10:4

Money has so much potential to make the heavens shift for you. Money creates a new beginning- a seed sown will attract new things to happen. Money is a great seed; if you want new things to manifest sow a seed of money. Money establishes your level. The amount of money you have will make people respect you or not respect you. It will open the doors that make you sit with the great and famous. Money gives you the ability to give to the poor

"He that has pity upon the poor lends unto the LORD; and that which he has given he will pay" Proverbs 19:17

Giving is lending to God. The thing is God owes, there is a note in heaven that says I OWE YOU and you can in the day of need Go before the LORD and ask for your money back.

Biblical Money Principles. Do not lend money and get interest from it unless you are a bank

"You are not to loan him money with interest or sell him food for a profit" Leviticus 25 vs. 37

A lot of people have built their empires upon the cries, sweat and labor of the poor. If you will make money the GOD way you cannot abuse people. If you use your tithe and you want to pay it back to God you will pay back with charges that amount to 20% Leviticus 27 vs. The love of money is a funny thing because people who love money are actually not people who squander. Money loving folks love to see figures and numbers in their bank accounts. They will keep and never spend. They will drive a ridiculously battered car, stay in a horrible house, sleep in tattered blankets but their accounts are bursting out with money. They love seeing the money; they accumulate it but don't spend it. Don't have the love of money, remember money is a tool.

How People deal with money?

The poor are consumers and will spend all their money on their stomachs. They don't think tomorrow they think today, they think only now. The Middle-class love to show off. Their clothes, their cars and their lifestyle are meant to show off to those they left behind. The Middle class have a semblance of I have made it. The rich are thinking generationally and they are the investors. Rich people think how to make money and will put effort there. Wealth people can lose money and will not be stressed because they understand they can and will make more money. Wealth people take risks; they are the biggest risk takers as they pursue making more and more money.

Wealthy people don't make noise but are silent as they don't want people to know they are wealthy. It's the poor who make a bit of money and they want the world to know they have money. Money is a spiritual entity that will either make you or break you. If you don't live by its principles, it will run away from you.   Money is a currency and as with any current it flows from a place of large concentration to a place of lower concentration.   If you don't locate the place where its coming from you will not have more of it.

CHAPTER THREE

ANCIENT TRUTH: PRINCIPLE OF SEED & WHEAT

I remember vividly this story as it was re told by a friend. The story is about two American missionary couples who went to Democratic Republic of Congo, then the nation of Zaire. The couples set up in a village that had a population of over five thousand people. They ministered for two solid years and none of the villagers came to the lord except for one small boy who then immediately got ex communicated from his family. In the second year the Lord blessed both couples and the wives fell pregnant, another couple had a baby boy and the other couple had a baby girl.

The baby girl's mother fell sick and died within a month of giving birth. The father of the baby girl out of pain and frustration he gave away the girl to the parents of the boy so they can adopt her and after burying his wife he flew back to America. He left the ministry and ended up an alcoholic. The other couple stayed for another full year in Congo without any progress then they came back home.

They now had three children. The African boy who was rejected by his family, their own son and the girl who had lost her mother and her father had left her. Years later the African boy and the white girl both graduated from university, the boy as a doctor and the girl as a missionary and they made the trip back to Congo together. The boy had a dream to build a big hospital to help his people. The girl had a dream to build a big church in memory of her late mother. Arriving in Africa they were welcomed by the amazed villagers. Months later the hospital and church mission had sprung up. The hospital was doing amazing things and so many people gave their lives to Christ by reason of the ministry of these two.

The girl flew to America and finding her father in a drunken stupor, she persuaded him to come with her to Africa. After all the protesting about why he should come and be reminded about his failure to bring the village to

Christ and him losing his wife in Africa, he eventually relented and came with her to Congo. Arriving in the village he was shocked to see a mega church of over five thousand people right next to his wife's grave. He couldn't understand how these two succeeded where he had failed. What the man had failed to understand was that God had sent him only to plant a seed. No matter what seed will manifest at some point. Seed will never die; it will grow and manifest.

The Principle of Seed and Wheat

"God said, let the earth bring forth grass. The herb yielding seeds and the fruit tree yielding fruit after his kind, whose seed is in itself" Genesis 1:11

Everything is a seed and everything that God created has a seed within itself. The principle works in human beings as well as in animals and in grass and herbs. The seed of anything is inside the DNA of that particular thing. It's imperative to understand that every kind of plant and all will create things after their kind. Human beings especially the male carries within them the spermatozoa which are a seed for the reproduction of human beings. The Maize seed carries within itself the ability to reproduce and have cobs that carry other seeds.

The ability to reproduce after its kind is within the seed.

"And I will put enmity between thee and the woman, and between your seed and her seed". Genesis 3:15

God then says it's interesting that the enmity between the devil and man is in the seed. What will fight the devil isn't the man but it's his seed. Without a seed you will not win the war. The only way any man can wage a war against anything and win is by reason of a seed.

The ability to identify a seed and sow the seed will give a man the opportunity to defeat the enemy.

"And Abel knew his wife again and she bares a son and called his name Seth: For God said she hath appointed me another seed instead of Abel whom Cain slew". Genesis 4:25

Adam and Eve saw Seth not just as a human being but a seed. Seth became the entity that reproduced and replenished what had been lost. Seed brings replacement and replenishment of what's lost.

"And behold, I establish my covenant with you and with your seed after you". Genesis 9: 9

The covenant of promise isn't only established by God to a man but also to his seed. Where ever a seed is there is the covenant established. What seed are you planting that can germinate and produce a harvest. What seed do you have that will create a harvest and that God can have a covenant with you on? Every man must have a seed and that seed is where the future lay.

"I will make your seed as the dust of the earth; so that if a man can number the dust of the earth, then shall thy seed also be numbered". Genesis 13:16

Thy Seed Not thy harvest is what God will make as dust. It's that seed that will take over the earth. The greatest challenge we have is that people look and see a harvest not a seed in the majority of times. Whenever we see a harvest, we eat all of it but whenever we look at what we have and see a seed we can take over the entire world. Your Church is the seed, the money in your pocket is the seed.

"All your seed shall be circumcised." Genesis 17:12

Seed has a special place in the heart and eyes of God so much that he wants it circumcised. Circumcision talks of separation and sanctification. It is to be made holy.

"In blessing I will bless thee, and in multiplication I will multiply you and thy seed as the stars of the heavens. And thy seed shall possess the gates of thy enemy". Genesis 22:17

The gates of your enemy, might be poverty, sickness or witchcraft can and will only be overcome by your seed. It's imperative that we all have seed. The gate is the entry point of anything, the place that gives the enemy entry is the gate. The bible then says the seed is what will take hold and possess the gate of the enemy. The stoppage of anything is a direct result of seed.

"I have been young, and now am old; yet I have not seen the righteous forsaken, nor his seed begging bread" Psalms 37:25

The seed can never beg for revelation because it's a natural thing that revelation will come by reason of seed. Bread is a daily need; bread is also an expression of revelation. Seed causes begging to cease.

"In the morning sow thy seed, and in the evening withhold not your hand; for you know not what shall prosper". Ecclesiastes 11 vs. 6

Prosperity is linked to your seed; any man that has nothing to sow shall never prosper. It's unfortunate that with seed it produces after its own kind. When you give a ridiculous seed, you will harvest according to what you have sown. The fact that you did sow once doesn't mean you stop, you keep putting your seed down because you don't know which seed will bring a harvest.

"For as the rain comes down and the snow from heaven and returns not without watering the earth and it makes it bring forth and bud that it may give seed to the Sower, bread to the eater". Isaiah 55: 10

The rain and snow come down to the earth that the earth can bud and produce. The earth actually gives to each as they need or desire, to one they get seed and they take over the earth, to another they get bread and they are excited because their needs have been met. It's interesting that the scripture actually says God gives bread to the eater and seed to the Sower. There are two things that you can get from God, either bread if you are an eater and seed if you are a Sower. Bread has so many interesting properties, firstly it's made of ground or pounded wheat, which simply makes it destroyed totally that it can never regenerate. Bread will remain fresh for a maximum of 7 days of which it becomes stale. But seed is for a lifetime as such the choice is all ours.

"When he sowed, some seeds fell by the wayside, and fowls came and devoured them up; some fell upon stony places, where they had not much earth; and forthwith they sprung up, because they had no deepness of the earth, and when the sun was up, they were scorched; and because they had no root, they withered away. Some fell among

Seed is many things, the word, its money, its ideas, and its revelation. Once seed has been released what's key is where the seed falls on. Its growth is determined by the place where it falls on. We must make sure we are the right ground for the falling of a prophetic word, for the manifestation of the word. Seed is usually soil specific, there is a seed that must fall on a prophetic conference and a seed that must fall on a Holy Ghost conference. The seed that's planted in Limpopo is different from the seed planted in North west province of South Africa because every seed is soil specific. Once a seed has been put in the right soil the seed will germinate and bring a harvest. Its then important to know the seed and the soil to plant the seed so that a harvest can come. Most people are disobedient and they just don't listen to God and they struggle because of that. The widow of Zarephath could have eaten one meal and died or could have just listened to the prophet and sowed the last that she had and lived forever on the little that was left. Most people struggle with the decision on what to do. You seed makes you or breaks you.

"The Kingdom of God is like a grain of mustard seed which a man took and sowed in his field: Which indeed is the least of all seeds: but when it is grown, it is the greatest among herbs". Mathew 13: 31- 32

The kingdom of God is a seed, the bible says that seed is small but it grows big. You cannot expect to start big; you can't start with a big church or a big business it will eventually grow. The concept of the Kingdom of God is a concept of seed. It's all a seed that is planted and gradually it grows. There are a number of factors in that verse, firstly it's a grain, secondly, it's a seed, thirdly the man took and planted it. Grains can be food or they can be seed, and the choice is up to an individual. The man took it and planted it. The choice to plant is in the parameters of human will.

"If your faith is as small as a mustard seed and you shall say unto this mountain (Mount Ebal- Mountain of curses) be removed and thrown into the sea it shall be removed nothing shall be impossible". Mathew 17: 20

Jesus was standing on the Mountain of blessing and he was pointing at Mt Ebal which is a mountain of curses. He then says that you can say to all the curses that be removed. Now the bible then says if your faith is as small as a mustard seed, you shall then speak to a mountain. The ability to speak to mountains is only given to seeds. Human beings can't address mountains but seeds can address mountains. Because seeds no matter how small have ability to grow and become gigantic and they will cause mountains to be removed and thrown into the sea.

"The Kingdom of God is as a man should cast seed into the ground, and should sleep and rise night and day and the

seed should spring and grow and he doesn't know how".
Mathew 4:26

The seed that's not cast down doesn't produce anything. Most people keep seed in their pockets instead of casting it down. Jesus is the seed of Abraham-

"If you are in Christ and Christ is in you then you are the seed of Abraham and heir according to the promise" *Galatians 3; 16*

Now we are the seed of Abraham so as God decreed to Abraham that his children shall be like the sand, we are what was decreed. We are born again of incorruptible seed by the word of God. 1 Peter 1; 23 we are a product of a seed.

"Whosoever is born of god does not commit sin, for his seed remain in him he is born of God" *1 john 3; 9*

The ability to overcome sin is in the seed that's on the inside of us. We carry the seed of God and it will germinate.

The process of the kingdom is a painful process. If anyone doesn't die as a seed they will not be resurrected as a harvest. Dying to self-will, dying to selfishness is not easy.

"When you plant a seed in the ground it has to die first it does not become alive again unless it dies first; If seed has to die for it to produce". 1 Corinthians 15:36 – 38

Most people do not want the dying process, because if God will use you then you must die to self, you must die to the flesh and die to self-will.

The process of wheat

You must put it into the ground, it has to die first. God will water it, then he will make it grow, God gives it a body, it will grow then be harvested by cutting the body and after cutting then the body will be thrown into the fire and what we want is the fruit which is the seed. The seed is taken to a threshing floor and they go through threshing, then grinding to remove the skin, then grinding to produce flour, then flour gets added water- washing of the water by the word

"That he might sanctify and cleanse it with the washing of the water by the word". Ephesians 5:26

Now Jesus had to go through the process so that he may be the Bread of Life. The bread that enjoyed by the world So God will take you through the process that the world may enjoy you

"Whatever a man so he will reap, don't be weary in well doing for in due season you will reap if you faint not". *Galatians 6 vs. 7*

Most times we fail to remember that there is a due season. They are a season where God will push full throttle for people to get a harvest for all their input. Be it money, be it adultery whatsoever seed that was sown there will be a harvest.

How a seed grows

Seed must be planted in soil, a seed on its own isn't productive, and it must be watered- washing of water by the word. Every seed is soil specific; it's got a certain soil that will bring manifestation of the seed. It needs air and a Seed Needs Light – Let there be light. The light of the word is needed to produce. Finally, a seed needs Proper Temperature.

CHAPTER FOUR

ANCIENT TRUTH: POWER OF PAIN

The man lay in Parirenyatwa Hospital for a good two years as the Doctors tried by all means to put his body back together. The excruciating pain that he was going was so unbearable that he had to be on a whole concoction of pain medications. Joshua had a call of the LORD over his life and for years had been refusing to go into the work of the LORD full time.

One day at work he had experienced an accident that left his hands, limbs and back bones all broken in different places. Miraculously he had survived this accident and after numerous operations he was finally able to sit in a wheelchair.

In his third year after the accident the LORD sent missionaries to his house who spoke to him about the call of God over his life. He ended up preaching whilst in a wheelchair, he did crusades but the pain was so un ending. He died five years later.

At one point or another of your life you will go through pain. Pain is inevitable, it's a part of life and can never be avoided no matter what. Pain is something that you will experience weather you love God and are doing all things right or you are not.

"And Jabez was more honorable than all his brothers and his mother named him Jabez saying because I bore him in pain" 1 Chronicles 4 vs. 9

Jabez had a name that was given to him by reason of the pain that his mother went through. Pain will come; pain will be there at one point or another.

Signs of Pain

Pain can be seen in a person's life by a number of things.

Crying and mourning- John 16 vs. 20 will always show that someone is in pain. Whether it is physical or emotional pain it will be shown by crying or mourning. Pain can be seen also by someone going through Agony and Grief. Most people going through emotional pain will not show it to the world.

THINGS THAT ARE PAINFUL

Pain can be physical and it can also be emotional, therefore there are so many things that can be painful some are physical and some are emotional.

Truth is painful- Job 6 vs. 25 "the truth can be painful, but what has your argument proven'.

The truth is extremely painful at times it's hard to accept the truth. The very fact that you are told things as they are is a bitter pill to swallow. It's easier for people to tell a lie because the lie will be more palatable than the truth. So many times, people cover up the truth and just say to someone what exactly they need them to hear. The challenge with lies is that when lies are spoken people make decisions based on the lies that have been spoken. When the truth then comes out it becomes a bitter pill.

Secondly Labor is painful; every woman when they get into labor they have to push because they know it's about time. The season will be there for a new thing to be born. The fact that it's now in season simply means it will and must come. It will without fail manifest though the process is painful. 1 Samuel 4 vs. 19/Galatians 4 vs. 19. Slavery is painful, and this experience can be better understood by people who lived through apartheid. Exodus 3 vs. 7. Circumcision is painful Genesis 34 vs. 25Circumcision is a process that was a sign of being covenanted to God. It was a process of cutting the foreskin. The process then entailed a separation of the Israelites from the gentiles. It meant that the old will be removed and the new will come. Circumcision is a painful process; it takes a while for one to heal from the wound of circumcision. Death of a loved one is painful as it totals separation. No matter how many times you have lost someone through death, you will realize that you cannot ever get used to the pain that comes from death of a loved one. When someone dies there is a pain that comes with it. Divorce is painful, as much as death is painful. The process of divorce will leave a lot of emotional pain, scars as one is separated from the person that they loved and had been joined to for a while.

Causes of Pain

Wickedness Job 15 vs. 20 *"The wicked person writhes in pain throughout his life, a number of years has been reserved for the ruthless"*

Pain always follows the wicked and no matter what they will have pain. Wickedness will open the door of pain; it will open the door that causes God to look away and not be the God of salvation. When you are in wickedness there will be pain, if wicked people surround you then pain will also come.

Giving birth brings with it pain, so before every harvest the labor is painful.

Psalms 48 vs.6 "trembling seized them there, pains like those of a woman in labor".

Giving birth is a painful process. The fact that a newborn is about to be born and released into the world simply means there is pain that will come with it. The fact that there is a destiny that's about to come on the earth simply means there will be pain that will follow.

Wounds cause pain – *Jeremiah 15 vs. 18 "Why is my pain unending and my wound incurable, refusing to be healed".*

Wound's weather physical or emotional is painful. Most people walk around with more wounds on them than what people can see. The wounds are emotional, the wounds are in their hearts and these will cause a lot of pain.

Bitterness causes emotional pain- *"When I chose to be bitter, I was emotionally pained" Psalms 73 vs. 21*

The fact remains that forgiveness is a choice given to all of us. We can choose to forgive and live right or we choose to not forgive and we end up with serious bitterness of the soul. Bitterness like it's always said is eating poison and expecting someone else to die. Bitterness is something that needs to be released. Lost opportunities will cause a lot of pain- I have been there were chances and opportunities will come but I lost all of them. These opportunities were lost as a result I went through a season of emotional pain.

Pregnancy brings pain- Isaiah 26 vs. 18

Struggles of Life will bring pain- Jeremiah 15 vs. 18

Thorns and briers cause pain- Ezekiel 28 vs. 24

Lack of kingly leadership and wise counsel cause pain - Micah 4 vs. 9

Diseases cause pain - Mathew 4 vs. 24/ Mathew 8 vs. 6

RESULTS OF PAIN

Pain is usually God's way of speaking, that something isn't ok and must be changed. Pain is God's way of taking us to another level. Pain has a number of things that it does.

Deliverance will come as a result of pain, so not all pain is bad.

"Be in pain, and labor to bring forth, O daughter of Zion, like a woman in travail: for now, shall you go forth out of the city. And there shall you be delivered". Micah 4 vs. 10

Pain sharpens your character- Without pain we never really amount to much. Pain will cause you to relook, rethink and re-strategize. Most things we do take for granted when we are in pain we will not do so. Pain will definitely bring you to a place where it changes your resolve; you will want change; you will want things to happen differently. When God allows pain, he allows it so that you may be shaped by it.

CHAPTER FIVE

ANCIENT TRUTH: WISDOM

"No mention shall be made of coral, or of pearls: for the price of wisdom is above rubies, the Topaz of Ethiopia shall not equal it, neither shall it be valued with pure gold, where does wisdom come from, where is the place of understanding; seeing it is hid from the eyes of all living, and kept close from fowls of the air" Job 28 vs. 18-20

"Wisdom is the principal thing; therefore, get wisdom; and with all thy getting get understanding". Proverbs 4 vs. 7

The two young excited prophets stood and began to confront this woman and asked her, "Mum what happened to this child, the woman said I don't know. The prophets then said you know, because you are part of a club of witches. You and your friends did this". To say a little, I would say that the woman was devastated, she was humiliated because these guys lacked a shred of wisdom, they just were unschooled and so uncouth. I have seen gifted people who are so blunt and lack wisdom in the execution of their gifts. Wisdom as the bible says is the principal thing.

Wisdom is an ancient science that has been established forever so much that the whole book of Proverbs is a book of wisdom. I will establish the importance of wisdom in this chapter. The first mention of the word prophet is in the book of

"And you shall speak unto all that are wise hearted, whom I have filled with the spirit of wisdom". Exodus 28 vs. 3

That they may make Aaron's garments to consecrate him that he may minister unto me in the priest's office

What is Wisdom?

Wisdom is the right application of knowledge, the ability to see what is not visible easily. Most people have knowledge of different things but they then fail to apply the very things that they know. The fact that you have read a manual does not mean you are able to apply what's written in the manual. It takes wisdom to be able to apply the things that you know.

Wisdom is a gift and it's a spirit. God actually imparts wisdom. It's the ability to judge a matter and the ability to make the right kind of decision. Wisdom is the ability to make the right decisions. Decisions wreck more havoc in people's lives more than demons and combined. When one lacks wisdom, they will find themselves in trouble. The ability to know the right path to take when you are faced with two paths before you are wisdom. It's the ability to have restraint in character. They are so many leaders who have no discretion, they live wreck less lives by reason that they are leaders. Wisdom is the ability to think as God thinks; it's the ability to see things the way God sees things. Wisdom is having that foresight, insight and hindsight that God has.

"Teach us to number our days, that we may apply our heart unto wisdom and the other version says teach us to count well our days. Then we will get a heart that thinks as God thinks". Psalms 90 vs. 12

As long as you cannot see things from the eyes of God you will not be able to judge the matter in the way that God does judge matters. It is having the eyes of your soul being like the eyes of God. Wisdom is also the ability to be artistic, the ability to design and to structure visible world. The ability to weave and build, every single person is somehow designing their world; you are putting structure and order into your own world. Wisdom does give you the ability to be artistic. The world around you is a direct result of your wisdom or lack thereof. It's imperative that we then must have wisdom to build our world.

"And I have filled him with the spirit of God, in wisdom, and in knowledge, and in all manner of workmanship". Exodus 31 vs.3

"And Moses called Bezalel and Oholiab, and every wise hearted man, in whose heart the LORD had put wisdom, even everyone whose heart stirred him up to come unto the work to do it". Exodus 36 vs. 2

Money is a result of wisdom; fools never make money. Whenever you see what a man is building it reveals his wisdom.

Signs of Wisdom

Peace in life is a sign of wisdom, the presence of chaos and lack of peace is a sign of lack of wisdom. Wisdom gives the ability to take the decisions that will bring calmness and peace all around you. It is the ability to synchronize things so that there is so much harmony in your life. Lack of peace is a sign of lack of wisdom.

"And the Lord gave Solomon wisdom, as he promised; and there was peace between Hiram and Solomon; and they two made a league together". 1 Kings 5 vs. 12

The ability to have people follow, listen and be part of what you are doing is in direct proportion to the wisdom that someone has in a particular area. People never follow fools; they follow a man's wisdom.

"And all Israel heard of the judgment which the king had judged; and they feared the king: for they saw that the wisdom of God was with him". 1 Kings 3 vs. 28

Wisdom brings respect and honor, people who are full of wisdom easily earn respect. People follow wisdom; the very fact that people are following you is a sign of wisdom. That's why in all thy getting you must get wisdom. Godly prosperity is a sign of Wisdom. God blesses wisdom. There is an unquestionable link between prosperity and wisdom

"Whoever obtains wisdom loves him, and whoever treasures understanding will prosper". Proverbs 19 vs. 8 ISV

Building a strong house, a strong marriage is a sign of wisdom- *"By Wisdom a house is built; it is made secure through understanding" Proverbs 24 vs. 3*

Wisdom is revealed by:

Wisdom is revealed also by the words of a man. Job has spoken without knowledge and his words were without wisdom. Job 34 vs. 35when a man opens his mouth it's easy to tell whether they are men of wisdom or they do lack wisdom. Wisdom as much as it is revealed by all these things above all it is shown by fear of the Lord and departing from evil,

Job 28 vs. 28 "The fear of the Lord, that is wisdom; to depart from evil is understanding

Wisdom brings respect and honor, people who are full of wisdom easily earn respect. Wisdom is in levels, it's not on one level. Not all wisdom is the same, some have wisdom for life, and some for business, and there are men who can speak in a few minutes something that will change your life forever.

"And Solomon's wisdom excelled the wisdom of all the children of the east country, and all the wisdom of Egypt". 1 Kings 4 vs. 30

The Egyptians then the Greeks were known for their wisdom, this was revealed by the building they did put up, the educational system they did set up and the systems of governance that they setup. Solomon did set up an awesome system of governance that even the queen of Sheba came and was shocked by what she found.

"And when the queen of Sheba had seen all Solomon's wisdom, and the house that he built, and the meat of his table, and the sitting of his servants, and the attendance of his ministers, and their apparel, and his cup bearers, and his ascent by which he went up unto the house of the LORD; there was no more spirit in her". 1 Kings 10 vs. 4 -5.

The systematic way in which things were set up was a revelation of the Wisdom of Solomon. The house of Solomon's design was a sign of wisdom, the amount of food at his table revealed wisdom and the systematic way in which his ministers did their things was a thought-out way.

Wisdom gives the ability and the strategies and to set up structures. The moment you see disorder, understand there is a lack of wisdom. Only wisdom can give the ability to put structures that are solid and will outlast you.

"And you, Ezra after the wisdom of your God that is in your hand, set magistrates and judges, who may judge all the people that are beyond the river". Ezra 7 vs. 25

It's easy to see a church that's led by a leader who doesn't have wisdom and an organization led by a leader full of wisdom, the systems, the structures and the way things are synchronized will reveal it all.

Sources of Wisdom

God is the source of all wisdom – *"For the LORD gives wisdom; out of his mouth comes knowledge and understanding" Proverbs 2 vs. 6*

"Multitude of counselors are a source of wisdom- Without counsel purposes are disappointed; but in the multitude of counselors, they are established" Proverbs 15 vs. 22

"For by wise counsel you shall make war; and in the multitude of counselors there is safety" Proverbs 24 vs. 6

"Where no counsel is, the people fall: but in the multitude of counselors there is safety" Proverbs 11 vs. 14

There is need for counselors around every individual, counselor in areas of money, marriage, leadership etc.

"Words of the Lord are a source of wisdom"- Proverbs 4 vs. 5

Get wisdom, get understanding; forget it not neither decline from the words of my mouth. Wisdom comes as an impartation from a prophetic voice or from a man that carries the gift.

"And Joshua the son of Nun was full of the spirit of wisdom; for Moses had laid his hands upon him; and the children of Israel hearkened unto him, and did as the LORD commanded Moses" Deuteronomy 34 vs. 9

Wisdom is present in ancient people- in old people. The fact that they have lived long, their experiences and their lives has exposed them to wisdom.

"With the ancient is wisdom; and in length of days is understanding" Job 12 vs. 12

Signs of a lack of wisdom

Not knowing when to speak – *"in the lips of him that has understanding wisdom is found; but a rod is for the back of a fool" Proverbs 10 vs. 13*

The words spoken, when they are spoken and how they are spoken is a sign of wisdom or a lack therefore.

Second sign of a lack of wisdom is indulgence into sexual immorality; this includes sexual orgies, rape, bestiality, incest, adultery, fornication and homosexuality. The third sign of lack of wisdom is mischievous behavior, it is a great sign of a lack of wisdom.

"It is a sport to a fool to do mischief; but a man of understanding has wisdom". Proverbs 10 vs. 23

Pride is a sign of lack of wisdom- *When pride comes then shame follows; but with the humble is wisdom. Proverbs 11 vs. 2*

Drinking alcohol is a sign of a lack of wisdom – *"They reeled and staggered like a drunkard, as all their wisdom became useless" Psalms 107 vs. 27*

"Because drunks and gluttons tend to become poor and drowsiness will clothe them in rags" Proverbs 23 vs. 21

Despising your neighbors and relationships is a sign of lack of wisdom- *"He that is void of wisdom despises his neighbors; but a man of understanding holds his peace." Proverbs 11 vs. 12*

When nobody listens to you that's a sign of lack of wisdom- *"People speak well about a wise man, but do not listen to a fool". Proverbs 12 vs. 8 EEV*

Why you need the ancient art of Wisdom.

1. You will only be able to build because you have wisdom.

2. Wisdom is a defense as money is a defense Ecclesiastes 7 vs. 12

3. Wisdom is better than foolishness as light is better than darkness Ecclesiastes 2 vs. 13

4. Wisdom makes your face to shine and gives boldness Ecclesiastes 8 vs. 1

5. Wisdom is better than weapons of war – Ecclesiastes 9 vs. 18

6. Wisdom gives you the ability to do the right thing. - Ecclesiastes 10 vs. 10

7. It is the same spirit that rested on Jesus Christ- Isaiah 11 vs. 2

CHAPTER SIX

ANCIENT MOUNTAINS

A mountain is a figurative expression of a congregation of people gathered around a Prophetic or Apostolic figure. Whenever we look at mountains, they were symbolic and also, they did have something that they meant. We will explore the different mountains that are in the Bible and also look at present day mountains. Every mountain in the bible represented a prophetic figure, a prophetic action or it represented a group of people.

Famous biblical mountains and what they represent.

Mt Ebal- Joshua 8 vs. 30-33/ Duet 11 vs. 29- Mountain of Curses, Ebal means bare mountain. Jesus is standing on mount Gerizim and he is pointing at Mount Ebal and he says you shall say unto this mountain be cast into the sea and if you do not doubt, but believe in your heart, it shall come to pass. Mark 11 vs. 23. Mt Ebal was a bare mountain that had nothing and it represented a place where curses were spoken, because they are cursed mountains that people go to. There are prophetic figures who don't carry the blessing but they carry curses. A lot of people go to false and fake prophets. These are represented by Mount Ebal, it also then represents demonic altars. It's that if you have faith you can speak to them and they will go. Every demonic altar will and cannot stand against you.

Mt Gerizim – Joshua 8 vs. 33/ Duet 27 vs. 12/judges 9 vs. 7- Mountain of Blessings - Gerizim means cutting off. Moses stands on Mount Gerizim and declares blessings to the children of Israel. The blessing of the lord comes only on those that are separated. It's the children of Israel whom upon the LORD then put a blessing upon.

Mt Hermon- Deuteronomy 3 vs. 8/ Psalms 133 vs. 3 Hermon was made famous by the psalmist when the spoke of the dew of Hermon. The word Hermon means a sanctuary, the mountain represents a sanctuary that carries a blessing. The blessing is attached to unity. Every mountain must be a mountain of unity for it to have a blessing.

Mt Ararat Genesis 8 vs. 4 Ararat means the Curse reversed. The ark of Noah lands on mount of Ararat.

Mt Pisgah – Numbers 23 vs. 14, Deuteronomy 3 vs. 27 Mountain of Vision. God says to Moses go on top of Pisgah and see the whole land. It is at Pisgah that the vision is very clear. It is the duty of Prophetic and Apostolic figures to make the vision clear.

Mt Calvary also known as Golgotha - Luke 23 vs. 33 / John 19 vs. 17 Golgotha which is mountain of the skull/ Mountain of sacrifice and deliverance. This is the mountain on which our LORD and Savior was sacrificed for the sins of the world. This mountain became the very place where the church in Jerusalem was established. This very place was the threshing floor of Arunah on which David built an altar unto the LORD.

Mountain of Moriah Genesis 22 vs. 2/2 Chronicles 3 vs. 1... On this mountain Abraham gave a lamb of sacrifice unto the LORD. Mount Gilead Genesis 31 vs. 25 Genesis 37 vs. 25/ Judges 11 vs. 29 Japheth of Gilead/ Jeremiah 8 vs. 22 the balm of Gilead. Means Rocky region nut in Gilead was healing. Mt Horeb Exodus 3 vs. 14 vs.1,

Deuteronomy 1 vs. 6 it's known as the Mountain of God. It means desert or desolate. Mt Sinai Exodus 19 vs. 11 and 18 / Exodus 31 vs. 18 / Numbers 28 vs. 6 Mt of God- Place where Moses received the law from God. Sinai means Thorny. The law became a thorn in the lives of the Israelites.

Mt Hour – Numbers 20 vs. 23- 27 It's a place of transfer of anointing and mantles. God spoke there and Aaron died there.

Mt Abarim Numbers 27 vs. 12 Abarim means regions beyond

Mt Zion- Deuteronomy 4 vs. 48 Zion means Monument or sign post it's the other name for Jerusalem, Judah was given Zion Psalms 78 vs. 68

Mt Seir Genesis 14 vs. 6/ Genesis 36 vs. 8 Land of Esau- shaggy or hairy

Mt Ephraim Joshua 19 vs. 50 Ephraim means double fruit.

Mt of Judah – Judah means Praise

Mt Olivet 2 Samuel 15 vs. 30/ Acts 1 vs. 12 David went unto the Mountain and he wept when Absalom rebelled against him. Olive which means Oil

Mt Carmel 1 kings 18 vs. 20 2 Chronicles 26 vs. 10 Uzziah had many vines in Carmel means Garden land

Mt Perazim Isaiah 28 vs. 21 Means Breaches, breaks God will do a strange work

Mt of Samaria- Amos 6 vs. 1Samaria was for Hellenic Jews the Word Samaria means Watch Mountains

Mt of Olives Zechariah 14 vs. 4, Mathew 21 vs. 1, 24 vs. 3, Mathew 26 vs. 30

In our present day there are special mountains that are known for their pull factor.

1.   Table Mountain

2.   Himalayas Mountain

3.   Mount Everest

4.   Nyanga Mountain.

What makes every mountain special is a number of features namely-

1. Its Visibility- How far and wide is it that it can be seen, and how far and wide are we advertising it?

2. Its density, the bigger the better so it's in the size of the mountain that it gains popularity.

3. Its pull factor, which is the key thing with Table Mountain. Every mountain has its attraction and that's the thing that needs to be put out to the world.

4. It's content as in the Great Dyke Mountains- we must be the church or business that everyone wants to be a part of.

The Table Mountain Effect:

Law of Marketing: There are so many mountains worldwide, they are humongous in size, and they are amazing in structure. But Table Mountain has nothing much to it but the shape of it. The South Africans have been able to package the mountain and been able to sell it to the world. Around the mountain a lot has been put that makes the mountain a must visit. The name has been made to be talked about so much, that it is an achievement to arrive at the Table Mountain. The South Africans keep talking about the mountain over and over and they don't stop. The same principle applies to churches and organizations. You may have a great Apostle or Prophet, but it's up to the owners of the mountain to market it. If the church doesn't market its gifting no matter how big and powerful the gift will never amount to anything. The Church needs a great marketing and media team. The better the marketing team the better the church.

Law of Value, the value of any mountain is the value that is given by the owners of the mountain. The moment they do not value it, then it loses value. Kilimanjaro, Table Mountain, Mount Everest and Nyanga mountains are some of the well-known mountains. There are many mountains out there, but these have been valued by the owners and they marketed them to the world. Value is only given by the owners.

Law of Protecting, Value and importance of any mountain is in how much the owners of the mountain protect the mountain. It's the duty of the church to protect the Prophetic and Apostolic figure. Every mountain becomes great by reason of how much the owners of the mountain firstly value the mountain. How much the owners of the mountain market the mountain. The Table Mountain has nothing to its name but the owners of the mountain have marketed their mountain.

Genesis 8:5 "on the first day of the month, where the tops of the mountain began to emerge again"

All mountains or Apostolic figure have their season of emerging. Most mountains then do not take advantage of their own season of emerging. They will be a moment when the mountains will be shown to the world and the mountains must therefore be revealed. It's important to maximize on the season of emergence. There are so many churches and so many men of God that have come up, they had their season and, in their season, they were the talk of town, they were pulling crowds and they were as if they are the only church in town. Then their season shifted, some took advantage and established systems that will give them money and pull people forever. In Zimbabwe we have seen major movements that arouse, to name a few;

Assemblies of God

Apostolic Faith Mission in Zimbabwe

Awake Grace Ministries

African Methodist Church

Christ Embassy

Celebration Centre

Family of God Ministries –

Glad Tidings Church

Methodist Church in Zimbabwe

United Methodist Church

Pentecostal Assemblies of Zimbabwe

ZAOGA Forward in Faith Church

Prophetic Healing and Deliverance Ministries

United Family International Church

These are some of the churches that became some of the biggest Pentecostal church movements in Zimbabwe and in the region. These Churches all had a season when they were the only church in town. They had a great pull factor, but eventually the tide died down and some have been able to keep up with what they established some did not. Some have been able to build churches, buy buildings, build schools and establish hospitals. Some did not establish anything tangible, but their season came and went. It's imperative to understand that times will shift and change. Every mountain must take advantage of its season and must then establish multiple streams of income. Every mountain must take advantage of its season to establish buildings and other ancillary things that will help it when another mountain has the pull factor.

MOUNTAINS BECOME

The Altar: *Genesis 12:8 "he moved into a mountain east of Bethel and there he built an altar"*- altars are built on mountains. Every Church is an altar of the LORD. It's a place of sacrifice; it's a place of contact with the spirit world. Every church must be a place of prayer, because prayer becomes the only thing that establishes an Altar.

Secondly, they become places of escape: Genesis 19:17 "escape to the mountain least you will be consumed" Every church has to be a refuge; Church is not just a place of spiritual experience but also a place of refuge. It is the center that the homeless, the poor and those facing challenges can go to.

Thirdly Mountains are places of serving the Lord: *Exodus 3:12 "you shall serve God upon this mountain"*.

Every prophetic figure in the Old Testament was attached to a certain mountain. It's then imperative that we understand that every church is a prophetic and apostolic mountain and upon it is an apostolic figure that is established there.

We do all that we can to market and speak about our mountain. Every Apostolic and Prophetic figure has a mantle that they carry that is meant to deal with a particular demonic system. For every Sodom there is an Abrahamic system, for every Jezebel spirit there is an Elijah anointing that must pull it down. The greatest challenge of God giving a man to us is that a man comes but he has his weaknesses.

According to Bishop Tudor Bismark, every mantle is then given three major things Grace, Rank and Influence. Every man of God has three things that he carries. The point is to bring you also to the place of influence. Grace, rank and influence are the three. We will look at these three.

Grace-is favor, elegance, acceptance in Greek its Charis which is the word Charisma and which becomes Charismata which is gifts. E very man of God has exceptional grace that they carry. This grace is also given to the people that are under him. We are Partakers of Grace- Romans 15:27, 1 Corinth 9 Vs 12. We all become partakers of the grace that is carried by the man seated upon the mountain.

The second thing that every prophetic and apostolic mantle carries is Rank –Its Place of power and operation 1 Samuel 3: 19 whatever word Samuel spoke never fell to the ground. Rank is easily mistaken for grace. Grace is the ability to operate and function, but rank is the authority that the man of Grace carries. Man can fall from grace but will never fall from rank; once a certain rank is attained it's attained forever. Rank simply is about what you own and it's about what you have achieved. Achievements happen over time, experience and increase in knowledge and wisdom gives rank. The last thing every Apostolic or prophetic figure carry is Influence. Influence is proportional to money, people and number of power gifts that submit themselves to you.

CHAPTER SEVEN

ANCIENT ALTARS

Foundations

"When the foundations are destroyed, what can the righteous do". Psalms 11:3 ISV

The Foundations can be destroyed, even for the righteous their foundations can be destroyed. The righteous can do something about it. This scripture is so amazing in that it establishes that you can be righteous and still your foundations are destroyed. The foundation of anything is the most important thing. The Foundation of a building is the anchor of that building. You then can be in the Lord and have broken Foundations.

Moses has foundational anger issues which are revealed by killing the Egyptian, then breaking the tablets of stones and by then hitting the stone and instead of speaking to it. It costs him the opportunity to enter the Promised Land he saw it but never entered.

Abraham lies that Sarah is his sister, so does Isaac and Jacob become the biggest liar. It's the issue of Foundations.

Japheth is a mighty man but his mother is a prostitute.

David says he was born in sin and we see sin following him.

"Behold I was brought forth in iniquity; and in sin did my mother conceive me". Psalms 52 vs 5

When you go into the background is a grandmother who was a prostitute. This manifests heavily on Solomon.

Majority of people struggle with things that were started by people that have long died and have gone. The Challenge lies in the DNA factor, it lies in the bloodline factor. It's a foundational matter. Till you are able to deal with foundation you cannot overcome.

"And they that shall be of thee shall build the old waste places: thou shall raise up the foundations of many generations; and thou shall be called the repairer of the breach, the restorer of paths to dwell in". Isaiah 58 vs 12

So, amongst us there is the ability to build Old Waste places. The foundation of Generations can be repaired and raised up.

Lamentations 4 vs 11; The Lord has accomplished his fury; he has kindled a fire in Zion, and it has devoured the foundations.

The first thing is God must devour the foundations, the evil foundations must be destroyed and devoured.

Hebrews 11 vs 10 For he looked for a city which has foundations, whose builder and maker is God.

There has to be a new thing, new foundation built and made by God.

Causes of Evil Foundations

- evil physical design

- envious rivalry

- evil dedication

- demonic incisions

- dream pollution

- demonic sacrifice

- exposure to evil diviner

- parental curses

- demonic blood transfusion

- demonic alteration of destiny

- demonic marriage

- evil laying on of hands

- fellowship with family idols

- inherited infirmity

- fellowship with local idols

- inherited infirmity

- fellowship with local idols

- demonic initiations

- unscriptural manner of conception

- fellowship with demonic consultants

- wrong exposure to sex

- destructive effect of polygamy

Galatians 3:13-14: Christ hath redeemed us from the curse of the law, being made a curse for us: for it is written, cursed is every one that hangs on a tree: That the blessing of Abraham might come on the Gentiles through Jesus Christ; that we might receive the promise of the Spirit through faith.

Colossians 1:13: Who hath delivered us from the power of darkness, and hath translated us into the kingdom of his dear Son:

Colossians 2:15: And having spoiled principalities and powers, he made a shew of them openly, triumphing over them in it.

2 Timothy 4:18: And the Lord shall deliver me from every evil work, and will preserve me unto his heavenly kingdom: to whom be glory for ever and ever. Amen.

The African traditional beliefs have so many ceremonies that border on demonic activities and then open doors to demons so they can operate in people's lives. These beliefs actually are sacrificial in nature. When we understand that Christ is the last lamb of sacrifice and any other blood sacrifice that happens is sacrilegious.

CEREMONIES

Masungiro Ceremony

There are so many African Cultural beliefs that we have crept into the church and have become part of culture and we have accepted them as if they are normal whilst they are open doors to the demonic world. Masungiro is basically the tradition that's done prior or after the birth of a child. The day a child is born he or she must be taken to the maternal parent's home. Masungiro is basically a COVENANT MAKING CEREMONY between the paternal and maternal families.

Masungiro means tying a child to the spirits from the mother's family and the father's family. Masungiro simply means tying someone to the ancestral spirit from his mother's side. Notice that this only happens to the first born, because the first always governs the rest. The ceremony of Masungiro happens so that there is a connection between the ancestral spirits of the paternal and maternal sides of the new born baby.

Masungiro requires a Goat or two goats and a cloth and a ceremony. On the day of Masungiro the Son in law must bring a cloth and leave it at the door and the mother-in-law must wake up jump the cloth and then she will clap her hands using the totem to thank the son in law and welcome the child into the family. Now this Covenant is a link between the spirits from the father and the mother. Every covenant requires a number of things

Symbol of the Covenant In this case it's the cloth and the Blood of the Covenant in this case it's the blood of the Goat.

These two things will seal the covenant and will make the covenant to be of effect on the life of the child. A number of things are wrong in this ceremony because it gives power to the demonic principalities to be connected and it does that with a blood covenant.

UMBILICAL CORD BURIAL CEREMONY

"Now as to your birth, on the day you were born your umbilical cord wasn't cut. You weren't washed with water to clean you, and nobody rubbed you with salt. And it's certain that you weren't wrapped in strips of cloth". Ezekiel 16:4 ISV

In most African cultures the umbilical cord once it dries up and it falls it must be taken to the family rural home and must then be buried there. The umbilical cord must not be buried anywhere else except the family lands. Unfortunately, with it being buried, so many destinies are also buried, so many stars are stolen at that moment. The umbilical cord is the first part of the human body that gets buried.

The greatest questions are?

1. Why do they want you to bring the umbilical cord to the village so they bury it? Why can't you bury it yourself?

2. Why is it given to these old grannies to dispose of it and not the parents of the child?

Was talking to a man who has been struggling with marriages and he said he discovered that people who did his circumcision at the village actually took the skin and used it for juju. So don't allow anyone to bury the umbilical cord. They are burying your child's future and yours

BURIAL CEREMONIES

Hair cutting ceremony at funerals: Most funerals especially of parents are where they will cut the hair of all the children and the elders bury the hair. All children of the deceased are supposed to have a cloth tied on their hands and the clothes will only be cut before burial and they must pay for it to be cut and the cloth is buried with the deceased. Something is sinister in this. Why tie the hands, hand talks of strength and money? You must pay for it to be cut. You are basically exchanging and paying them to take your strength.

They bury the clothes basically they decree and bury your destiny. Why would people Cut hair when the Bible is straight that Hair is Glory? It's the Glory of Elders, it's the Glory of Women. Cutting of hair and burying it is burying the Glory of the Children

"Gray hair is a crown of glory; it is obtained by following a righteous path. Lastly Parents learn to bath your Children". Proverbs 16:31 ISV

Even a day old and also be the first that cut their hair. Do not leave this to some old Grannies from the village.

"Pay attention, now! I am sending you out like sheep among wolves. So be as cunning as serpents and as innocent as doves". Mathew 10:16 ISV

"The glory of young men is their strength; and the splendor of elders is their gray hair". Proverbs 20:29 ISV

"Nor that hair is a woman's glory, since hair is given as a substitute for coverings". 1Corinthians 11:15 ISV

We allow our children to be in the hands of people that mess up their destinies. We will be dealing with deliverance issues. We have so many foundational issues that delay us.

FAMILY ALTARS

"Then the angel of the Lord commanded Gad to Say to David that David should go up and set up an altar to the Lord in the threshing floor of Onan the Jebusite." 1 Chronicles 21: 18

1. It is simply a place of contact with the spirit world.

2. It is also a place of sacrifice and a place of Covenant.

In the Old Testament, when God gave the promise of a land to Abraham, he quickly built an altar of prayer on the land and sacrificed to the Lord.

Ancient altars first follow, Bloodline- the enemies of a person shall be those of his household.

Every family has a family altar. The altar may be righteous or an unholy altar. Every church, every religion has its own altar. The pulpit and our offering baskets are our altar that's why we don't share the altar. In most families they have rural homes. Have you ever noticed that in the rural home there is the round hut? In the round hut there is a place they call CHIKUVA- its straight-forward it's the Tomb. CHIKUVA- is the place they use when they are doing African traditional Religion. They put a plate there and worship the ancestors. Same place is used when they are doing lobola ceremony. Same place is used when they are having the body of a deceased person to lie in state. That place is the family Altar and it's the place they use also for Lobola ceremony.

If the family isn't using the rural home there is one particular house, they use to do lobola. Why they do that it's because it's the very place that has been established as a family altar. And they will definitely use it to connect with the dead. In the New Testament however, an altar is simply a place of contact with our God we are no longer commanded to build physical altars Unto God, only spiritual ones. It is just simply a particular place at a particular time of the day when and where an individual child of God Meets with his Maker. The Old Testament altar was made of stones and wood but now, the Word teaches us in:

"God is a Spirit (a spiritual Being) and those who worship Him must Worship Him in spirit and in truth John 4: 24

The Altar of David

"Then the angel of the Lord commanded Gad to Say to David that David should go up and set up an altar to the Lord in the threshing floor of Ornan the Jebusite." 1 Chronicles 21: 18

Anytime God sought to covenant with humankind, to sanctify, pardon, or set free, an altar was usually raised to bring this into effect. In the above scripture, pestilence and tribulation had been in the land and thousands of men and women were already dead or dying.

"And David built there an altar to the Lord and offered burnt offerings and peace offerings and called upon the Lord; and He answered him by fire from heaven upon the altar of burnt offerings. Then the Lord commanded the [avenging] angel, and he put his sword back into its sheath." 1 Chronicles 21: 26-27

When God smelled the peace offerings and the burnt offerings from the altar, His anger abated and mercy and compassion took over. If you are having pestilence, destruction, or divine judgment in your community, the answer is the altar

KINDS OF ALTARS

1. Your house or wherever you pray and have a regular encounter with God is a form of altar.

2. The family altar –where the family gathers together for prayer.

3. Your Church is another altar as it is a place of prayer, sacrifice and worship.

4. Special conventions and Conferences where there are prayer rooms become citywide/national/international altars.

Other Satanic Altars

Statues –there are statues and monuments erected which look ordinarily like works of art but have spiritual implications. Most governments erect these monuments to celebrate events or certain individuals that passed away.

Many festivals celebrations in the guise of tradition and culture are basically times and seasons of negotiations and transactions with the powers of darkness. In Shona culture there are festivals like kurova guva which is basically a memorial service. These have a ceremony that includes men sleeping at the graveyard by the grave of the deceased and they will kill a Goat and they will immerse its head into a clay pot of traditional beer. The moment it dies they will cut it and drink the fresh blood and they cut out the liver and eat it uncooked. A number of things are wrong with the ceremony, people are at the graveyard, secondly killing a goat at the graveyard, drinking blood and eating uncooked meat.

There is also the issue of satanic blood covenants through incisions. They are made on people's bodies by native doctors who are witches or agents of witches.

Three major things happen through incisions: nyora

1. There is a blood covenant.

2. Incantations are made before or during the incision which are coded words that are curses.

3. A black substance is rubbed into the body through the incision which of course is the entry point of demons into the person's life. All these blood covenants with Satan through tribal marks, incisions and body.

Marine Altars/Water spirits

White garment altars and Mermaid altars. Marine altars are built in rivers, the sea, dams, or any body of water. Names and images of people can be dropped into various bodies as well as images of people. And as long as the water covers that object, the progress of the individual concerned will remain covered. His or her progress is subsequently submerged and they say, "As this thing that is thrown into the river can never float, so the man will never come up to the top, the man will never rise to the top, his progress will never be seen." White garment prophets always have water reeds or water from different places that they place on their altars.

White garment churches -Forest Altars

There are a lot of people whose destinies get tied up in the forest. White garment priests and witch doctors actually give people clothes that they go and tie in the trees and they will be tying destinies. You usually see around a body Parts representation before Altars. Body parts from people have been commonly used as a means to afflict people. By body parts we refer to such things as urine, hairs, feces, fingernails, menstrual pads, etc. That is one reason why women have to be careful about how they dispose of their menstrual pads.

We have heard of witches, sorcerers, and satanic agents that go round dustbins pretending to be looking for food but actually looking for menstrual pads, which they would take to altars. The blood of a woman is in the pad representing her reproductive ability. They make incantations and speak some curses on those things and whomever the woman is that is involved, may be rendered barren or she may have many female problems. She may even experience difficulties in the area of marriage. Placentas are also taken to an altar and rituals are performed. The mother and the baby may suffer many troubles and afflictions in life and not understand what the root cause could be. Clothing Altars They can take clothing to altars. That is why we must be very careful about our clothes. Everything that has contact with our bodies or which are from our bodies, can be taken to these places and then used to afflict.

PURPOSE OF DEMONIC ALTARS

Altars are used to make contact with the Spirit

World – Genesis 8:20-21. Sacrifices are made at the altars in order to make contact with the spirit world, with demons, (evil spirits) and territorial powers. In the Old Testament, the people of God erected or built altars in order to make contact with the Living God. An Altar is a Place of Invocation of Evil Spirits –Genesis 12:8. An altar is a place for invoking evil spirits, once the necessary sacrifices have been made.

Sacrifices are tokens given to the demons to request for their assistance in afflicting people. No witch will fight you physically, no wizard will take you on physically, and they do it spiritually. And all they do at the altar is to invoke evil spirits for help after giving them token sacrifices. This is one of the purposes of the altar. There, people contact the services of demons for help. In order to operate and function in the spirit world, man has to function dependently. No human being can function independently in the realm of the spirit. Even as Christians, we have to function dependently before we can really deal with our enemies. We have to depend upon the Holy Spirit and God's angels who use our words, (PRAYER) as it were, in order to attack the powers of darkness. That is why the Bible says we wrestle not against flesh and blood and that the instruments of our warfare are not carnal but MIGHTY through God. So, we too, have to function in the spirit realm dependently.

Altars are used to monitor the Progress of People.

Once your name has been submitted at an altar or your image is there or they are using a crystal ball or a satanic mirror to monitor you, wherever you are, they can influence your life. Whether you are in America, South Africa or Australia does not matter. Once they call your name and your name or image appears on a mirror, they can see how far you have gone, the progress you are making and then they can begin to encumber you. There could also be agents of the altar that physically come to visit you, like as baby-sitters, house maids, gardeners and even friends, who only come to spy for your enemies and take the report back to the altar priests.

Altars are used to Destroy People.

The end result of every altar of affliction in a life of a man is his destruction. Little wonder then, the Bible says in

John 10:10 that, *"The thief does not come except to steal, and to kill, and to destroy."* Satan is a destroyer and he uses satanic altars

MANIFESTATION OF ATTACKS FROM SATANIC ALTARS

How do I know that an altar has been erected against my life? How do I know that something is operating against my life? Maybe an image altar, a name altar, a pictorial altar or an astral altar how do I know that one form of an altar or the other is operating against my life

What are the symptoms?

Here are a few indications. Some of what we suffer in life can come as a result of Curses or spells, and some as a result of ancestral covenants. An altar is the satanic operational headquarters where a lot of negative things are released against the lives of men, women and children.

1. Repeated Tragedies and Delayed Blessings.

If a person has a regular, repeated tragedy especially at the point of breakthrough.

2. Sickness.

There are people who fall sick exactly the same time every year, they also can fall sick same time every month. These sicknesses may surpass generations. Some of these sicknesses that we call generational sicknesses are actually a result of an altar speaking against you. I have met people who they whole family has diabetes or hypertensive. The sicknesses from one generation to the next generation.

3. Irrational behavior

There are people who do things they can't understand. The moment they have money they will become uncontrollable and they will be having irrational behavior and this will only stop when they have lost all the money, this is a result of an altar. There are ladies that the moment they meet a good guy they will reject him and will then leave and after he is gone then they will start thinking well.

4. Death Wish and Suicidal Tendencies.

The word says I came that you may have life and have it more abundantly, and it is a right to live long. The devil comes to steal, kill and destroy, and he will push some people to kill themselves, he will push some people to the edge. Every time someone has suicidal thoughts and tendencies that is a sign that there is a spirit at work and in most cases a result of a demonic altar. The devil wants so many people to be in hell with him, so he will definitely do everything to have many people die before they have given their lives to Jesus Christ.

5. Abnormal Losses.

There was a family I ministered to; every night money would be withdrawn from their bank accounts. This happened for some time and they ended up monitoring and the bank checking cameras but nobody was taking their money. It was spiritual, and therefore was a spirit that was stealing money. Altars have a tendency of stealing money from people.

6. Mysterious Body cuts

You sleep at night and by the time you wake up; you discover that all kinds of marks and lacerations have been made on your body. This is the work of evil spirits from hell to tamper with your blood and health. They have used satanic needless to inject you and to draw blood. This is usually the cause of serious sicknesses. When one begins to see fresh and mysterious body marks, sometimes emitting blood, one has to do something very quickly.

OTHER AREAS THAT SHOW FOUNDATIONAL SPIRITS

A number of Ministers Struggle because of the following things, someone was a Sangomas in your family - they opened a door way in the family that allows the devil to claim legal rights. Jezebel became the open door of a cause over Ahab's Family. This Verse is interesting. It says if the Righteous not the unrighteous. If the foundations be broken there was blood shade in the family. Believe it demons only operate on legal ground. The moment they have legal ground they will operate and claim. Once you hear these stories you need to deal with this curse

You are the First pastor in your family. Because you are the first you are breaking a furrow ground it will be hard. But all the ones coming after you will definitely have it easy. Jephthah was a valiant soldier but something kept lingering on that he was born out of wedlock

The fact that there was ancestral worship in the family

The fact that someone went and took a foreign God so they can get money. You were born out of wedlock. You will deal with the Bastard spirit. Challenge with the bastard spirit is that you are not supposed to settle down in any area of life and not to make it in any area. The greatest struggle comes from Foundations.

When you were born who received you and who spoke first words to you. Your surname is someone name. One man who mentored me did a research on his surname and found out that it had been changed and it was but because the grandfather was always asking out young ladies out and they had then given him a new surname that became the permanent and registered surname. I have seen men who are praying for miracles and for people to get money but themselves are struggling badly in life and ministry

"Now Jephthah the Gileadite was a valiant soldier, but he was also the son of a prostitute and Jephthah father Gilead". Judges 11:1 ISV

I have met Men who are great preachers and powerful on the pulpit but their churches do not correspond with the labor they are putting. You got cursed by A Parent- be biological or Spiritual. That opens a door of struggle in life and ministry. You are carrying a name that speaking evil against you. How can you succeed if you are a serpent so we get named after an uncle and an aunt who never have made it in life what do you expect?

Belinda means Bright snake what your name means.

Names like Tambudzai, Nhamo, E.g., will be blockage to your future. No matter what you do they will control you, sharing a name with someone you basically living the person's life? You will go through the Person struggles. We love to call our children names. We call them David if you see them having may women and falling because of them it's the name

Who named you and what does your name mean?

Is a feminine given name of unknown origin, apparently coined from Italian belle, meaning "beautiful"? Alternatively, it may be derived from the Old High German name Belinda, which possibly meant "bright serpent" or "bright linden tree". Linda means snake, what your parents were saying whilst you were in your mother's womb. Some of us need to change names. I had to change one lady name from Tambudzai to Tania. Now we have seen progress in her life. Dig deeper around your Name and Surname what do those two names mean the seed was sown at foundation of the pregnancy. Let me touch more into rejection, the spirit of rejection can cause;

Money can reject you

Ministry rejects you

Marriage rejects you

The land rejects you.

These things can reject you because they have a spirit of rejection. The spirit of rejection is a foundational demon that comes because;

1. Your father refused you whilst you were still just in the womb

2. Your mother may have tried to abort you as a baby.

3. Your family rejected you for one reason or another.

Already the spirit of rejection is following you. It will follow you forever. You will be rejected by people, rejected by money and rejected by the ministry; you may be the righteous one of God but have a foundation that's broken. Foundations will speak on your behalf no matter what you do they will speak. You may never go far because there is something speaking. You will struggle to go far with life but there is hope at the end of the tunnel. Like we said if the foundation be broken what can the righteous do.

1. We should all dig into our past. Who were your great grandfather and mother from both sides? What did they struggle with, find your history it will enlighten you?

2. What INIQUITY did they Struggle with and also Dig into Names, what does your surname mean and where did it come from. What does your name mean? You may need to change the name

E.g., is there a history of:

1. Divorce

2. Polygamy

3. Sickness e.g., Diabetes, High Blood Pressure

4. Failure

5. Ancestral worship

5. Consulting White garments

 If there was then you must begin to break these things

CHAPTER EIGHT

ANCIENT LANDMARKS

Remove not the ancient landmark, which thy fathers have set. – Proverbs 22 vs. 28

We grew up in a family that basically had roots of coming from a lineage of kings and chiefs. The family hailed from a place called lower Gweru. Our fore fathers eventually because of continuous droughts and challenges in that area later moved from lower Gweru to an area then known as Sipolilo now Guruve. The area that was under their jurisdiction in Lower Gweru remained unoccupied to present day. It has been proven that anyone who is not of our bloodline if they move into that area and try to settle all kinds of misfortunes will befall them and they eventually leave. This is a clear sign of ancient landmarks.

Joshua proclaims a curse upon Jericho and he says "cursed in the presence of the LORD is the man who restore and rebuilds this city of Jericho, He will lay its foundation at the cost of his first born and at the cost of his youngest he will set up its gate" Joshua 6 vs. 26

Joshua sets up an ancient landmark. The Ancient landmarks are a basically territorial mark that puts boundaries on places. They become marks ownership and also mark of limitations to how far one can go.

Curse is translated to be an annoyance, to irritate to be a nuisance. The first mention of the word curse is in;

Genesis 3 vs. 14 "You are cursed above all cattle, and above every beast of the field; upon your belly shall you go, and the dust shall you eat all the days of your life"

The second curse that God gives is to the ground.

"Cursed is the ground for thy sake; in sorrow shall you eat of it all the days of your life" Genesis 3 vs. 17

The third mention of a curse is to Cain,

"And now you are cursed from earth, which opened her mouth to receive your brothers' blood from your hand" Genesis 4 vs. 11

Curse basically is a number of things

a. It is the removal of the blessing, the grace, the protection of God on a place, a person or an object.

b. It is the authorization of a demonic oppression and possession over an individual, a family, a place or even an object. There are individuals that are cursed; they carry the curse over their lives. They basically struggle through life, businesses or marriages. There are families that are cursed, they will never have peace, and all the individuals in the family have a set barrier that they will not be able to pass no matter what. There are nations that carry the curse because nothing the nation ever tries to do will rise.

There are places which are cursed; these places will not produce anything. They are barren, they are totally unproductive. You will find houses that are cursed, lands that are cursed and spots that are cursed. Majority of these spots end up being accident spots and people continue to die in these places.

"Put the blessing upon mount Gerizim and the curse upon Mount Ebal" Deuteronomy 11 vs. 29

Meroz is cursed declared the angel of the LORD. Utterly and totally cursed are its inhabitants, because they never came to the aid of the LORD Judges 5 vs. 23

"Jesus redeemed us from the curse of the law becoming a curse for us" Galatians 3 VS 13

Then there are objects that are cursed, these maybe clothes, money, objects. In African culture they had a practice of taking a goat to a priest who would then pronounce a curse removed from the family and put on the goat. The goat would then be released into the wild. If anyone ever took the goat the curses would follow them. The same process would happen with money. They would release a curse on the money and they would throw it on a cross road. Whosoever would pass by and then see the money and pick it, the curse would jump on them. Curses are transferable from place to place, individual to individual.

SIGNS OF EXISTANCE OF A CURSE

Misfortunes that come one after another and you can't explain the source of those misfortunes.

"Jehovah will send upon you cursing, discomfort, confusion and rebuke, in all that you put your hand to do, until you are destroyed, until you perish quickly" Deuteronomy 28 vs. 20

Repeated challenges, it maybe sicknesses, money challenges and any other misfortunes. Death that happens at a certain time of the month or at a certain month in the year.

Failure to conceive and give birth as children is a blessing from the LORD. Every time you face situations that are anti the blessing. General bareness in life. The city will reject you- Deuteronomy 28 vs. 16. Your children will struggle, and anything you start will struggle- Deuteronomy 28 vs. 18

SOURCE OF CURSES

'Like a fluttering sparrow or a swallow in flight, a curse without a cause will not come" Proverbs 26 vs. 2

There are no curses that just come they come because there is a reason or there is a place that they are hanging on to. We will look at the different sources of curses. God himself will curse people and places and objects that go against his principles. When a group of people do things that are contrary to the word, the LORD will release a curse.

Secondly Idol worship of any kind will cause a curse to be released.

"Cursed be the man that makes a graven image, an abomination unto the LORD" Deuteronomy 27 vs. 15

Idol worship includes worship of graven images, worship of ancestral spirits and all that is ungodly. Thirdly the devil and his agents, witch doctors, false prophets and all in his kingdom specialize in cursing and curses upon people so that they may destroy destinies. This way they control lives and they destroy lives,

"The thief came to steal, kill and destroy and I came that you may have life and have it more abundantly". John 10 vs. 10

Fourthly, stepping upon cursed ground brings curses, because there are lands and places that carry curses. Fifthly Parents can curse their children some knowingly some unknowingly, by speaking negative words upon them curses will come. Parents have power to curse because they are a life source, when you don't honor them, you will be cursed.

"The moment you curse your parent you shall die". Exodus 21 vs. 17

The Moment you dishonor your parent you are cursed.

Incestuous relationship is a source of curses, Deuteronomy 27 vs. 22. Some curses like these just come upon you the moment that you engage in these illicit affairs.

Bestiality produces a curse, Lastly, when you fall into sin it opens the door of curses.

BREAKING CURSES

Your offering will break a curse: "I will not again curse the ground anymore for man's sake" Genesis 8 vs. 21.

Offerings are a spiritual transaction that can break the power of curses. Offering is a seed that is sown and by reason of that curses will be broken. David builds an altar on the threshing floor of Arunah and the curse gets broken.

Secondly, Bless Israel the nation of God and the curses will be broken.

"I will bless them that bless you, I will curse them that curse you" Genesis 12 vs. 3

The third way a curse will be broken is for you to be blessed by God himself, you will be above any curse.

"How shall I curse, whom God has not cursed, how shall I defy whom the LORD has not defied" Numbers 23 vs. 8

Fourthly, When the LORD loves you then the curses will be broken.

"The Lord turned the curse into a blessing unto you, because the LORD your God loved you" Deuteronomy 23 vs.

THE ART OF WITCHCRAFT

Witchcraft is magic, sorcery (bewitchment), enchantment (attraction), and spell casting. The art of witchcraft is an ancient art that has existed since time immemorial. The art of witchcraft is meant to do a number of things namely;

1. Manipulation- some people end up in marriages that they didn't plan to be in and they don't understand how it happened. Then there are parents who live their dreams through their children, they failed to be medical doctors but they will manipulate their children to become doctors not because their children want to but it is just the dream of the parent. There are mother in laws who do not let go of their sons they still want to control and manipulate them and they do fight with their daughter in laws all the time.

2. Witchcraft is destiny control; it is meant to control the future of an individual.

3. Witchcraft is Destiny Delay- delayed goodness, delayed marriage, delay in receiving good things. You will receive them way beyond the time that you must.

4. Witchcraft is Destiny destruction- you feel you must be in England but you in Zimbabwe and as much as you maybe in a place somehow you know you are in a wrong place.

Galatians 5: 20 Witchcraft is a work of the flesh. It's then a result of fleshy desires. Witchcraft is a direct result of envy that leads to covetousness. Witchcraft used to only be about stopping your destiny, it has evolved over time it doesn't stop you from getting it just gives you the wrong thing.

Wrong husband – a spouse to totally frustrate you instead of your real spouse who will enhance you.

Witchcraft will give you a Wrong business that will frustrate you in every direction. Witchcraft will give you a Wrong Job that will never be a blessing but a curse. Witchcraft basically takes you out of your God ordained place.

1. Witchcraft originates from Lust and it will give room to envy and that will open a door to jealousy and becomes covetousness then finally Witchcraft.

2. Witchcraft works through Personalities to control municipalities. There has to be a jezebel that comes in the family. Witchcraft works through one or two people in the family who are then used to be the contact point.

3. Witchcraft works through ancient altars and ancient landmarks, Witchcraft is magic, sorcery(bewitchment), enchantment(attraction), spell Only the Kingdom of God can counter the demonic and the witchcraft kingdom.

CHAPTER NINE

ANCIENT RIVERS

The river of Kishon swept them away, that ancient river, the river Kishon. O my soul, thou have trodden down strength. – Judges 5 vs. 21

Rivers are a flow of water; it is the currency of the river that makes the river to be known and to be powerful. Rivers are a symbol of the spirit. Rivers chart their own course depended on the power of its currency. There are men of old who know the way to bring revivals, they have walked the road. There are ways that will bring revivals, bring a move of God and a touch of the power of God. Eli in spite of the fact that he is rejected of God, he speaks Hannah's miracles into manifestation, and he mentors Samuel to hear God.

Life is a wrestle; you will have to fight to get to the place of manifestation of your miracle. Most people get to the place of giving up, they give up and they lose their miracles.

People will go through struggles in life, at one point or another you will struggle through life.

Why people Struggle in Life

Bad Choices in areas like investments, Marriage and courses to take. Everyone has the Gehazi moment, that moment that will define you forever it's the time where you must go right but may end up going left. It's the turnaround moment that can turn out to be the worst moment. Choices decide the future, choices decide what will happen now and in the future. Most struggles in life are a result of bad choices.

People struggle in life by reason of complacency. Complacency is simply the moment people get into a comfort zone. Mostly people fail to develop themselves and fail to go to the next level because they become comfortable with where they are, so much that they don't develop further. Life is dynamic, businesses are dynamic and they change all the time and when one fails to develop and move with the times they will struggle on the next level.

Lack of Knowledge is the next biggest reason why people struggle. Whichever area in your life that's an area of darkness will eventually lead you to a place of struggle. Whatsoever you don't know becomes a weakness.

Lack of honor – Once there is a lack of honor there is a lack of blessing. Joshua is the only man that gets the hands of Moses laid on him. He receives this grace because of serving Moses.

"And Joshua the son of Nun was full of the spirit of wisdom; for Moses had laid his hands upon him, and did as the Lord Commanded MOSES". Joshua 34 vs. 9

Unwillingness to submit to the fathers is another reason why people struggle. You can never be in authority unless you are under authority. God will not bless disorder but he blesses order. People struggle in life because they don't have a strong will power. Will power give the drive, it gives the push that's needed for one to be able to accomplish in life. Lack of Integrity is a major reason why people struggle in life. If you can't be trusted with tithe of 1000 dollars how can God trust you with 1 million dollars? Integrity is the measure of your corruptibility risk. If you can easily be corrupted then you will struggle in life. God is a God of principles and by reason of that he honors his word.

Lastly people struggle because of demonic Oppression and attacks will bring you to a place of non-achievement.

Paul writes and says in

"Are they Hebrews? So am I. Are they Israelites? So, am I Are they the seed of Abraham? So, am I" 2 Corinthians 11 vs. 22?

Paul says he is a Hebrew and the word Hebrew means a dream chaser, a river crosser. We are dream chasers; we are river crossers. So as river crossers we will face challenges and trials along the way to achieving what we desire. Isaac is moved from Gerar because the king was jealousy of his prosperity. Isaac reopens his father's enterprises. The first well was Esek which means dispute, so he left it, second well was Sitnah they fought him for it and he left it also. The third Well was Rehoboth –which means The Lord has given us room and we will flourish. Finally, after struggling two times Isaac finally God makes room for him. In life you will wrestle with yourself, you will wrestle with decisions, you will wrestle family traits, you will fight divorces and failures, and you will fight the propensity and proclivity to lean towards sin. Dream chaser, river crossers, vision bearers, glory cloud carriers have the greatest struggles in life.

You will have a great message but nowhere to preach, great song but nowhere to sing, it will seem everyone is doing well except you. The key is in keeping on doing the right thing. Genesis 11vs 30 Sarah is barren but Hagar had a child. Genesis 25 vs. 21 Isaac entreated the Lord for his life because she was barren and the Lord was entreated of him and Rebecca his wife conceived… and two nations are in her womb. Esau and Jacob in *Genesis 29 vs. 31 and when the Lord saw that Leah was hated and he opened her womb but Rachel was barren. Genesis 29 vs. 32 LEAH gives birth to REUBEN- SEED- unstable as water sleeps with his father's wife*

Genesis 29 vs. 33 LEAH gives birth to SIMEON – he is an instrument of cruelty

Genesis 29 vs. 34 LEAH gives birth to LEVI so is Levi an instrument of cruelty

Genesis 29 vs. 35 LEAH give birth to JUDAH – he is praise but has no discernment sleeps with his daughter in law.

30 vs. 1 Rachel is still struggling to have children.

30 vs. 3 Rachel gives BILHAH give birth to DAN – is a snake, a viper by the road.

30 vs. 8 Rachel gives BILHAH gives birth to NAPHTALI- Free running animal that has children everywhere

30 vs. 11 LEAH gives ZILPAH and she give birth to GAD- Bandits will raid him and he will raid back

30 vs. 13 LEAH give ZILPAH and she gives birth to ASHER- his food is delicious he is a food person

30 vs. 18 LEAH give birth to fifth son and she calls him ISSACHAR- a strong donkey under two burdens, a slave at forced labor

30 vs. 20 LEAH give birth to the sixth son calls him Zebulon– his place is the periphery

30 vs. 21 LEAH give birth to a daughter DINAH.

30 vs. 22 And God Remembered RACHEL and she gives birth to JOSEPH and then BENJAMIN

Though Leah, Bilhah and Zilpah are producing children what they are producing isn't quality children but still Rachel is struggling. The fact that someone is producing doesn't mean what they are bringing out is quality. Abraham has no children but lot has but what he is producing isn't quality. Quality takes time

There is nothing that is of quality that happens overnight. Time is the best measure of quality. Quality products take time to produce. Quality products usually become antiques.

There are things that are an ancient way and they will always be that. It's the way things flow; things take time and quality things will take time.

CHAPTER TEN

ANCIENT TRUTH: THE KINGDOM, THE POWER AND THE GLORY

The Kingdom of God is a spiritual kingdom; it's not a physical kingdom. Its mandate is spiritual and its manifestation is physical. It is therefore a Kingdom that's meant to exert its system and ways upon the earthly kingdom. We are spirit beings who have a soul and we live in a body. Our mandate is then to manifest the kingdom of God. Therefore, the kingdom of God is on the inside, it's in us, as we walk, we are in the kingdom and the kingdom is in us.

It's then our mandate to manifest the kingdom. Because we carry the kingdom and the mandate of the kingdom in these earthly vessels, the enemy will try by all means to attack the very vessels that are carrying the Kingdom.

The Kingdom of God is therefore in the Holy Spirit. If we remove the Holy Spirit, we do not have the kingdom of God at all. The Kingdom of God is manifestation of power".

The Kingdom of God being spiritual is always wresting against the demonic world. The reality of the spiritual world cannot be disputed. The fight between the Kingdoms is about territory. The devil wants territory. The devil will do a number of things but top above that will release demonic assignments.

Every demonic assignment is meant to do a number of things. Demonic assassination- exterminates the growth of the kingdom of God, physically, spiritually and numerically. It will assassinate gifted people so much that they will never amount to anything; this is the reason why gifted people have the greatest struggles in life. Jeremiah the prophet is always crying till he says, the reason why I am preaching is only because your word became like a fire unto my bones. Demonic vexation - You can be vexed in your mind, body, spirit or finances. Demonic assignment targets Divine Assignment. Where there is no divine assignment, you don't find demonic assignment. For every Abraham there is a Sodom, for every Elijah there is a Jezebel, for every John the Baptist there is a Herodias who wants to cut off your head.

Demonic limitations these limitations are so much meant to stifle growth. These demonic landmarks will stop progress in life. Landmark mark demarcations on how far someone can go, these can be the case of lack of church growth, lack of growth financially and any other growth in life. There are families that have never owned land, never owned a car and some have never ever been able to fly in an aero plane. These are all signs of demonic limitations.

Signs of Demonic Assignments:

Lack of Peace

Lack of financial progress

Lack of general Progress in life, business or ministry

Delay- it's stolen time that cannot be recovered. It's a missed Kairos moment that drags the Kronos moment

Sickness

Defeat by enemies

Your past keeps following you.

Vexations by demonic powers- *'O Lord, son of David have mercy, O lord: My daughter is grievously vexed with a devil'. Matthew 15 vs. 22*

"Lord, have mercy on my son; he is a lunatic, and sore vexed; for oft times he falls into the fire and often times into the waters". Mathew 17vs.15

"There came also a multitude out of the cities round about Jerusalem, bringing sick folks, and them which were vexed with unclean spirits; and he healed everyone". Acts 5 vs. 16

Every Gift carrier has a Divine assignment. What the devil is after is the gift not the carrier of the gift. He then will eliminate the carrier so as to mutilate, destroy and completely decimate manifestation of the gift. No gift can function outside the confines of the carrier of the gift. No matter how powerful a gift is, it will not at all work without being any part of the embodiment of a person.

How to deal with Demonic Assignments

"So shall they fear the name of the LORD from the west, and his glory from the rising of the sun. When the enemy shall come in like a flood, the Spirit of the LORD shall lift up a standard against him". Isaiah 59:19 KJV

God raises a standard that's against every demonic assignment. The kingdom of God is a spiritual Kingdom and as such it requires one to be spiritual. Its operation is spiritual as well. So, when the flood of the enemy comes then comes also the spirit will raise a standard.

"And in the days of these kings shall the God of heaven set up a kingdom, which shall never be destroyed: and the kingdom shall not be left to other people, but it shall break in pieces and consume all these kingdoms, and it shall stand for ever". Daniel 2:44 KJV

The demonic kingdom operates for a limited season and time, but the Kingdom of God is eternal.

"And he sent them to preach the kingdom of God, and to heal the sick". Luke 9:2 KJV

The operation of the kingdom of God will be forever and ever, and as the kingdom is preached its power is demonstrated.

"For the kingdom of God are not in word, but in the demonstration of power". 1 Corinthians 4: 20

"Now about that time Herod stretched forth his hands to vex certain of the Church; he killed James the brother of John with a sword. And when he saw it pleased the Jews, he proceeded further to take Peter also... Vs 5 Peter therefore was kept in prison; but prayer was made without ceasing of the church unto God for him". Acts 12 vs. 1

The Lord has prepared his throne in the heavens, and his kingdom rules forever." Psalms 103 vs. 19

"Repent for the kingdom of heaven is at hand". Matthew 4 vs. 17

"But seek you first the kingdom of God and his righteousness and all these things will be added" Matthew 6 vs. 33

Keys of the Kingdom

"The Kingdom has got keys that can lock and unlock things. Whatsoever you bind on earth is bound in heaven". Mathew 16 vs. 19

It's the power of the kingdom. It's the power to control the spiritual and the same way control the natural. The word says the children of darkness are wiser than the children of light in that they have understood the fact that there are keys to the supernatural.

Blessed are you Simon Barjona for flesh and blood has not revealed this to you. The Kingdom of God comes only by revelation. It's never something that comes by recognition. The challenges in life are a result of a Lack of revelation.

Jesus and all the important things in the kingdom are not recognized it is only revealed. That's why someone can be in a church and be poor; someone can be in a place and never get the benefit of the place. Jacob sleeps in a place and he sees angels ascending and descending from heaven. Some people slept there and never saw anything but a man with revelation sees the heaven.

Revelation is a result of inspiration and inspiration a result of manifestation of the gift of the Holy Spirit.

Revelation becomes the rock on which the church is built.

The gates of hell can't prevail against revelation. The gate of hell prevailing against you is a result of lack of revelation. The Moment revelation comes then immediately there is ability to overcome the devil.

Mysteries of the kingdom – Luke 8 vs. 10 unto you it is given to know the mysteries of the kingdom of God; but to others in parables.

The kingdom is a mystery, it's hidden in a mystery- The Kingdom has gifts hidden in mystery and revealed in time.

Gifts hidden in Kairos and revealed in time. God is the mystery that he being God gets into the womb of Mary and is born like a human being and is revealed to men. He who knows their God shall be strong and do exploits. To know God, you must know Jesus and to know Jesus you must know the word. Because Jesus is wrapped in the word it's the bread of life that you must eat. If you don't eat the bread, you can't have the energy to go on.

Luke 9 vs. 62 "and Jesus said unto him, no man having put his hand to the plough and looking back is fit for the kingdom of God".

Luke 12 vs. 31 "but seeks first the kingdom of God and all these things shall be added unto you."

1 Corinthians 4 vs. 20 "For the kingdom of God is not in word but in the demonstration of power."

The Armies of the Devil that fight the Kingdom

Gates of Hell – Psalms 18 vs. 5 "the sorrows of Hell compassed me about: the snares of death prevented me."

2 Peter 2 vs. 4 "For if God spared not the angels that sinned, but cast them down to hell, and delivered them into chains of darkness, to be reserved unto judgment."

Revelations 1 vs. 18 "I am her that lives and was dead; and, behold, I am alive forevermore, amen; and have the keys of Hell and of death".

Hell is the place that has been set up to bind the devil and his demons. It's the very pit that carry all evil. The gates of hell figuratively become the very entry point into the kingdom of the devil. When the gates of hell are set up against you, then you will face all demonic attacks and trails.

Walls -2 Samuel 22 vs. 30 "for by thee I have run through a troop; by my God have I leaped over a wall."

Demonic walls are basically blockages on the path of an individual, these walls will close the way and these walls will stop progress in the life of an individual.

Troops – Job 19 vs. 12 "His troops come together and raise up their way against me, and encamp round my tabernacle."

Demonic troops are a council of wickedness, these may be enchanters, covens of Satanists that rise against the righteous ones of the LORD.

CONCLUSION

There are truths that are, they were, that will always be. We may fight, disagree or disapprove but these ancient truths will outlive civilization. God bless you.